WITHDRAWN

RESTRUCTURING SCHOOLS FOR COLLABORATION

SUNY Series, Educational Leadership
Daniel L. Duke, Editor

RESTRUCTURING SCHOOLS FOR COLLABORATION

Promises and Pitfalls

Edited by

DIANA G. POUNDER

State University
of New York
Press

Published by
State University of New York Press, Albany

Production by Susan Geraghty
Marketing by Nancy Farrell

Printed in the United States of America

For information, address State University of New York
Press, State University Plaza, Albany, N.Y., 12246

Library of Congress Cataloging-in-Publication Data

Restructuring schools for collaboration : promises and pitfalls /
    edited by Diana G. Pounder.
        p.   cm. — (SUNY series, educational leadership)
    Includes bibliographical references and index.
    ISBN 0-7914-3745-0 (hc : alk. paper). — ISBN 0-7914-3746-9 (pb :
alk. paper)
    1. School management and organization—United States. 2. School
-based management—United States. 3. Community and school—United
States. 4. Educational change—United States. I. Pounder, Diana
G. II. Series: SUNY series in educational leadership.
LB2806.R396 1998
371.2'00973—dc21   97-25123
                                                                      CIP

10 9 8 7 6 5 4 3 2 1

CONTENTS

ACKNOWLEDGMENTS

Thanks to my departmental colleagues and contributing authors for their tireless efforts, cooperation, and good humor; to my department chair, David Sperry, for his solid leadership, ethics, and even-handed nature; and to our devoted staff, including Ms. Jamie Burton for her superior skill, effort, and attention to detail in the manuscript production.

CHAPTER 1

Introduction and Overview
of the Book

Diana G. Pounder

Collaborative work organizations have become the focus of both research and practice in business and industry during the 1990s. This focus is appearing in research and practice in education as well. For example, the conference programs of recent American Educational Research Association (AERA) and University Council for Educational Administration (UCEA) have focused on collaboration and related themes such as community, cooperation, and so forth. Some may view emphasis on collaboration (or community) in schools as the second stage of the initial "site-based management" movement initiated in the late 1980s. School organizations have begun expanding their democratic governance emphasis with teacher, parent, and community advisory councils; engaging in partnerships with other human service agencies or businesses; or redesigning educators' work to add a group or team emphasis.

Most scholars focus on only one particular type of collaborative work arrangement—such as school-business partnerships, industry-education collaboration, regular education-special education collaborations, or even schools as "learning communities." Further, they view the study of collaboration through a single conceptual or disciplinary framework or lens. For instance, personnel administration experts tend to use a social-psychological framework to study collaboration or other group efforts. Other educational administration authorities may use organizational theories, political or micropolitical lenses, economic frameworks, leadership theories, or theories of teaching and learning to understand the success (or failure) of collaborative organizational efforts. However, because collaboration may increase the complexity of organizing and

1

managing, a single lens, framework, or disciplinary approach is an inadequate aid to understanding such complex organizational phenomena. Further, when building collaborative schools, practicing administrators and teachers need to consider multiple factors such as: (1) What organizational structure will enhance collaborative school efforts? (2) What change processes are important in building school collaboration? (3) What are the costs (in effort, energy, time, or other resources) of collaborating with other external agencies? (4) How can teachers' work be redesigned to enhance collaboration among teachers and what are the outcomes for teachers and students? (5) How can educators (e.g., administrators, teachers, special education teachers, counselors, psychologists) overcome their separate role socializations to build collaborative work relationships within schools? and (6) What are the implications of school collaboration for teaching and learning, school leadership, and leadership preparation? Thus, this book presents chapters that discuss collaboration research and practice from multiple perspectives. Specifically, the book includes chapters which discuss each of the following:

1. The structural considerations that are critical to school collaboration; uses an organizational theory framework (Johnson, chap. 2)

2. The change processes necessary for collaborative schools; uses an organizational change and development lens (Barott & Raybould, chap. 3)

3. Collaboration between schools and other human service agencies; uses an organizational economics framework (Galvin, chap. 4)

4. Redesigning teachers' work to have a collaborative team emphasis; uses a group work design approach (Pounder, chap. 5)

5. Collaboration between and among educators in different roles (e.g., teacher, counselor, principal, special education teacher, social worker); uses a role theory and professional socialization perspective (Hart, chap. 6)

6. Implications for instruction; uses teaching-learning literature (Evans-Stout, chap. 7)

7. Implications for school leadership; uses leadership research (Crow, chap. 8)

8. Implications for preparing educational leaders; draws upon knowledge and experience from a collaborative educator preparation program (Matthews, chap. 9)

Each chapter is authored by a member of the Department of Educational Administration at the University of Utah, and, as such, is a collaborative work effort itself. Our interest in writing a book on school collaboration probably has a couple of sources. First, like many researchers, we perhaps had some interest in this topic due to our own professional experiences with work collaboration. We have experienced successful and not-so-successful collaborative work dynamics as well as highly collaborative and highly isolated work environments. Why has our department been able to engage in a decade or more of successful collaborative endeavors and to maintain healthy colleaguial dynamics in spite of faculty turnover and other departmental changes? And why have some other departments had to struggle to come to consensus, to share common goals, to work together successfully in spite of earnest efforts to do so? We did not have many answers to these questions. Further, as we began work on the book, we realized that little empirical work exists to address the nature of effective school collaboration; much more of the literature on school collaboration is conceptual or even ideological.

Second, our interest in collaboration was stimulated by several informal discussions between and among department faculty over lunch. As we exchanged our ideas and observations, we realized that each of us focused on collaboration through different disciplinary and experiential lenses. And, that it is the combination or integration of these multiple perspectives which may have greatest potential for explaining effective collaborative efforts.

Each chapter author has professional and scholarly expertise in a particular disciplinary area. These areas include organizational theory (Bob Johnson), organizational change and development (James Barott and Rebecca Raybould), organizational economics (Patrick Galvin), group work design and personnel administration (Diana Pounder), work roles and professional socialization (Ann Weaver Hart), instructional leadership (Karen Evans-Stout), leadership and the school principal (Gary Crow), and leadership preparation (Joseph Matthews). Thus, the book comprehensively addresses the topic of school collaboration with a multidisciplinary approach.

CHAPTER CONTENTS

The book is organized into three major sections: (1) foundations of collaboration—organizational structure and organizing change process considerations, (2) different types of school collaboration—interagency collaboration and intraschool collaboration of teachers and educators in multiple roles, and (3) implications for instruction, leadership, and educator preparation. The book progresses from more broad or abstract understandings of organizations in the early chapters to more specific and concrete considerations and implications of restructuring for school collaboration in the later chapters. The chapters discuss conceptual issues and considerations relevant to collaboration, report research findings, and present the "promises and pitfalls" for practice in collaborative schools. The content of each specific chapter is elaborated in the chapter descriptions that follow.

In chapter 2, Bob Johnson examines the ways we organize schools—how schools divide, coordinate, and control the work done. Just as the halls in a building direct and define the flow of traffic in the building, so the structure of an organization directs and defines the flow and pattern of human interaction in the organization. Given the structure of most schools, what patterns of interaction are being defined, enhanced, or hindered by this structure? How do these patterns of interaction facilitate or inhibit collaborative efforts? Additionally, Johnson discusses the nature of the core technology of schools—teaching and learning. He argues that "form should follow function" and that because the teaching and learning function of schools has fairly high levels of ambiguity and equivocality, schools have a higher need for communication and the exchange of ideas among workers than do some organizations—thus a greater need for work collaboration. Lastly, he discusses several features of schools that should be considered in organizing for collaboration: (1) the stimulus-overload, labor-intensive nature of school environments, (2) the autonomy norm which defines the teaching profession, (3) the pupil-control theme inherent in schools, and (4) the vulnerability of public schools to their environments.

In chapter 3, Jim Barott and Rebecca Raybould examine the nature of change in organizations and the implications for organizing for school collaboration. They discuss collaborative change issues of interdependence versus professional autonomy or discretion, collaboration versus conflict, and costs versus benefits. They also address the tension between change and persistence, discussing the distinctions between first-order change and second order change. First-order change refers to change that occurs within a system and allows the basic nature of the system to persist. Changing organizational members is an example of this type of change; the people are new, but the positions and duties are the same. Second-order change transforms the system, altering the basic nature of the organizing system. This second type of change requires a change in the group's assumptions or rules of relating or interacting.

The authors further outline some of the problems, difficulties, and impasses that may result with first- and second-order changes. Lastly, they discuss some of the promises and pitfalls of changing schools into collaborative organizations.

In chapter four, Patrick Galvin, using economic theories of organization, examines the nature of interagency collaboration between schools and social service agencies. He traces the history of failure of educational and social services as well as the history of interagency collaboration dating from the 1930s. He then offers an economic explanation for the shortcomings of many collaborative efforts— largely those of costs such as coordination costs, foregone opportunity costs, information costs, and ownership/monitoring costs. He argues that the demise of some collaborative efforts may be a function of rational decision-making to reduce collaboration costs rather than of a lack of commitment to the ideology or goals of collaboration. He closes with recommendations for changing governmental incentives to encourage or allow effective collaboration between schools and other social service agencies. Galvin's conceptual analysis is especially intriguing because it uses a framework (economic) that many of us neglect in our analysis of social interactions such as those occurring in collaborative endeavors.

In chapter 5, I discuss how teachers' work can be redesigned to have a work group or team emphasis. I argue that the educational experiences of students can be less fragmented and more holistic if delivered by an interdisciplinary teacher team rather than individual teachers addressing separate subject matter and curricular areas. Addressing group structural elements including job characteristics (e.g., discretion, skill variety, feedback) and work group composition, the chapter presents a conceptual framework for effective work groups or teams. The model also addresses organizational context factors and healthy interpersonal process considerations. Using the model as an organizing framework, I review research on interdisciplinary teacher teams in schools, concluding with an analysis of the promises and pitfalls of interdisciplinary teacher teams engaging in work collaboration.

In chapter 6, Ann Weaver Hart provides a conceptual, empirical, and practical look at the functions, challenges, and outcomes of intraschool collaboration among educators holding different professional roles (e.g., school teachers, counselors, psychologists, social workers). She argues that collaboration among the professionals who work in schools marshals a more complete professional resource toward the achievement of educational goals and the solutions of educational problems and that educators need a broader understanding of one another's roles and functions and the tools of collaborative problem-solving in order to maximize their joint impacts on children and youth. The chapter is organized around four themes: (1) professional work roles in school, including role concepts, role functions, and role socialization; (2) the social structure of professional work groups; (3) conflict management; and (4) collaborative problem-solving.

In chapter 7, Karen Evans-Stout addresses the implications of collaboration for instructional practice. She (1) synthesizes what we know about instructional collaboration from past efforts, (2) discusses some of the known promises and pitfalls of collaboration for instructional improvement, (3) analyzes the changing context of education and some of the tensions of teaching and learning that have implications for instructional collaboration, and (4) offers some recommendations for those considering collaboration as a means to foster instructional improvement. In particular, she argues that recent instructional goals emphasize teaching for in-depth understanding or student-centered learning in a rich authentic context; that is, learning as knowledge construction. This type of instruction may require teachers to negotiate certain day-to-day teaching-learning interactions and tensions in ways that are more easily done privately than publicly/collaboratively. These and other contextual factors must be considered when restructuring schools for instructional collaboration.

In chapter 8, Gary Crow considers the implications of collaboration for school leadership. The chapter examines the expanding nature of leadership in collaborative schools—the quantity and spheres of leadership. He discusses the influence and systemic nature of leadership and collaboration and follows that with a review of relevant literature on the expansion of leadership roles and leadership in school reform settings. The chapter concludes with a discussion of implications of school collaboration—its promises and pitfalls—for school administrators in particular.

In chapter 9, Joseph Matthews discusses the importance of and need for training more administrators and other educators to work in more collaborative school settings. In particular, few school administrators have had any formal training and practice in teaming, collaborating and consulting. They are often ill-equipped to function with other educators, parents, and support staff in a collaborative culture. Matthews argues that those who wish to collaborate effectively must study, model, and rehearse specific methods and practices both at the pre-service level in preparation programs and at the in-service level for practicing educators. The chapter then describes a specific training program developed at the University of Utah to train administrators and other educators in different professional roles to work collaboratively with one another in school settings.

In the closing chapter, chapter 10, I offer a synthesis of the major issues and dilemmas that cut across the previous chapters. These dilemmas are framed as collaboration's "promises versus pitfalls"—or opportunities versus challenges for schools. The synthesizing issues include: (1) the need for change toward more collaborative schools versus the tendency of schools to persist in traditional approaches to education, (2) resource gains versus costs of collaboration, (3) professional interdependence versus professional autonomy or discretion (and the related concepts of independence, privacy, and isolation), (4) shared influence (or leadership) versus shared accountability (or responsibility), and (5) balance of influence versus overcontrol or underinvolvement among collaborative parties.

INTENDED USES

We hope you find the contents of this book useful, informative, and thought provoking. Our intended audience includes education professors (especially those in educational administration, teacher preparation, and social and cultural foundations) and school practitioners (especially school administrators and teachers). In addition, district-level administrators, education policy-makers (e.g., school board members, state office of education leaders, and state legislators), professional support personnel (e.g., school counselors, psychologists, or social workers), and perhaps social service professionals or other human service professionals involved in interagency collaboration may find the book's contents relevant to their work.

For academicians, the book provides multiple disciplinary perspectives for understanding the "promises and pitfalls" of school collaboration efforts. The book may inform research by providing research findings and implications for practice from different theoretical or conceptual frameworks. The book chapters also discuss multiple types of collaboration (e.g., interagency collaboration and intraschool collaboration) that are not included in most single textbooks. Thus, the book provides a more comprehensive discussion of collaborative school efforts than any other single source we could find. It also informs cross-disciplinary teaching in colleges of education and offers specific guidance on the design of preparation programs emphasizing collaborative schools. The book has the potential to be a primary or secondary text in any number of education courses, including school restructuring, school change or organizational change and development, school leadership, teacher leadership, schools as organizations or organizational analysis, educational policy studies, educational planning, human resource administration, or a basic introductory course to educational administration.

For education practitioners, the book presents a logical organization of major considerations in school collaboration initiatives: the organizational structure, the change process, interagency and intraschool collaborative efforts; and implications for instruction, leadership, and leadership preparation. Further, the book provides practitioners with a concise presentation of research findings from organizational, change process, economic, social-psychological, sociocultural, instructional, and leadership literatures on school collaboration.

Whatever your interest, we hope that we have offered an array of perspectives on school collaboration that inform you and stimulate your consideration of collaborative efforts in education.

CHAPTER 2

Organizing for Collaboration: A Reconsideration of Some Basic Organizing Principles

Bob L. Johnson, Jr.

Whether in reference to the individual, group, or organization, discussions regarding the need for increased collaboration in American public education appear to be on the rise. A cursory review of the literature attests to this growing interest. One reads of the need for increased collaboration among teachers in planning instruction (Pounder, 1997); among teachers, administrators, and parents in school governance (Malen, Ogawa, & Kranz, 1990); among schools and businesses in the pursuit of support and funding; and among schools and other public agencies in the delivery of social services (Johnson & Galvin, 1997). It appears that talk of collaboration along a number of topical fronts is *au courant*.

Several factors account for this growing interest. Foremost among these is the call for greater democratization in the workplace, a call rooted in the political ideology which defines American culture (Bailyn, 1972; Dahl, 1956; Dewey, 1916). From an ideological standpoint, collaboration is sought for collaboration's sake: it is the *democratic* thing to do. The communitarian sentiments reflected in the work of Etzioni (1993) and Bellah (1991) are indicative of this collaborative movement and spirit.

Closely aligned with this ideological factor are the values reflected in current decentralization efforts witnessed in both public- and private-sector organizations. Though often promoted under the guise of increased workplace democratization (Greenberg, 1975), such efforts tend to be driven by more pragmatic values, most notably the values of effectiveness and efficiency. As has been noted by Johnson and Ellett (under review), and in the context of public- school organizations, decentralization and the concomitant need for increased collaboration are viewed as important means for increasing school effectiveness and productivity.

Given the ideology implied in the act of collaboration, the perceived productivity dividends associated with it, and the tendency of reform debates to be co-opted by the latest trends and ideas (Cuban, 1988), it is not surprising that calls for increased collaboration in public education have emerged. For many, the move toward greater collaboration within and between schools represents an important means of addressing a wide variety of educational problems (Johnson & Galvin, 1997). Such enthusiasm, however, is not entirely unexpected (Kingdom, 1984). As with many new or rediscovered initiatives, rhetoric often outruns the realities. Of greater interest are questions regarding the workable realities of collaborative initiatives in schools. What do we know about collaboration in organizations? What conceptual frameworks can assist us in understanding collaborative efforts in schools?

As a means of addressing these important questions, this chapter seeks to articulate the principles and assumptions that guide the ways we might think about organizing (Weick, 1979) through a *reconsideration* of two important organizational concepts. The larger context of the arguments is rooted in ideas drawn from the field of organizational theory, but the specific context of application is the school organization. Two concepts guide the discussion which follows: (1) the current *structure* of schools and (2) the *core technology* of schools.

RECONSIDERING ORGANIZATIONAL STRUCTURE

A reasonable point of departure for considering collaborative efforts in schools is organizational structure. What is organizational structure? What functions does it serve?

In the most generic sense, structure may be defined as the way an entity is patterned or arranged. The word-picture associated with its Latin root (*structura*) is that of a building. More specifically, it is a building as defined by the individual components used in its construction *and* by the relationships shared between these components as configured in the construction process. Hence, the structure of a given entity, that which identifies it as unique, is defined by two aspects of the entity itself: (1) the individual elements of which it consists and (2) the way in which these elements are patterned and configured, that is, how they relate to each other. For example, water is a unique substance that has two components, hydrogen and oxygen, bonded together in relationship of two atoms of hydrogen to one atom of oxygen. It is these individual components *and* the relationships shared between them—that is, the configuration of these individual elements—which define the unique structure of that entity known as water.

Although an etymological analysis of *structure* may appear somewhat removed from discussions of organizations, the logic and ideas associated with it have some utility for understanding the relationship shared between the structure of an organization and the level and character of collaborative efforts which occur in it. This utility becomes evident as one considers the definitions of structure offered in the organizational theory literature (Scott, 1992; Hall, 1991; Morgan, 1986; Ranson, Hinings, & Greenwood, 1980; Mintzberg, 1979; Blau & Schoenherr, 1971). Although a review of the varied definitions of organizational structure is beyond the scope of this chapter, two specific definitions are offered for consideration.

Mintzberg (1979) defines structure as "the sum total of *ways* in which [organizational leaders] divide [the labor of organizational participants] into distinct tasks, and then achieve coordination among [these tasks]" (emphasis added). In a manner similar to that observed with the Latin derivative, Mintzberg's definition implies the existence of individual components *and* of patterns and relationships among these components. Implied is the assignment of sets of work-tasks to individuals, roles, or groups and the relating or coordinating of these work-tasks toward some larger end. Scott's definition mirrors that of Mintzberg's. Scott defines organizational structure as "that set of features that arises as a result of the efforts within the organization to differentiate the labor; and coordinate and control the work" (Scott, 1992, p. 227). However, in contrast to Minztberg, Scott extends the functions served by organizational structure to include that of controlling organizational behavior.

While both definitions may be criticized for their hyper-rational overtones, a substantive measure of conceptual validity is contained in each. Considered together, organizational structure is defined here as the ways (patterns) in which the work within an organization is divided (components) *and* in which coordination and control over this work is pursued (relationships among components). It is these *patterned social features* which define the structure of an organization.

While this conceptualization of structure raises many questions about the relationship between organizational structure and collaboration, an initial question which must be addressed, and one which defines the purpose of this chapter, is as follows: How does the concept of structure help frame one's thinking about current efforts to increase collaboration in schools?

Insights regarding the answer to this important question can be found in the works of Weick (1979), Simon (1981, 1976), and Barnard (1938). Concerned more with *the act* of organizing rather than the organization itself, Weick argues that organizing and strategic planning represent attempts at retrospective sense-making. That is to say, organizing and strategic planning represent afterthoughts rather than forethoughts. According to Weick (1979), an organization comes into being *after* individuals (or occasionally a sole individual) come to the realization that the task they wish to complete is beyond their capabilities (Simon, 1976). Upon this realization, the group is faced with two choices: (1) cease to consider engaging in the task altogether or (2) seek to collaborate with others in completing the desired task. For Weick, this second choice—choosing to collaborate—is known as *organizing*. It occurs *after* the group identifies a task it wishes to complete and *after* it realizes that this task cannot be completed alone.

This view of organizations and the organizing process presupposes organizational purpose.* Though the degree of specificity of this purpose may vary across organizations, organizations may be considered purposive entities. This view likewise presupposes the existence of a collaborative and coordinated effort among multiple individuals. It is in this sense that organizations may be considered coordinated, collaborative entities. The importance of collaboration in understanding organizations is reflected in Barnard's (1938) classic definition of the formal organization as a "system of consciously coordinated activities of two or more persons" (p. 73). Though the extent of collaboration and coordination may vary from organization to organization, the basis of organization is *coordinated collaboration*.

In light of this conceptualization of organizations, organizational structure, and the organizing process, it is necessary to consider the role structure plays in defining the patterns and character of collaborative relationships which develop in organizations. Fundamental to this understanding is the realization of the artificial nature of the formal organization (Simon, 1981).† In contrast to such naturally occurring phenomena such as trees, animals, plants, water, and so forth, organi-

---

* While there are debates regarding the existence and functions of organizational goals, it is argued here that organized behavior is purposive. In making this claim, one not need assume that this purposive behavior is formally stated or made explicit.

† Realizing the conceptual pitfalls surrounding discussions of human organizations and their origins, I take great care to include in this statement the adjective *formal* to describe the type of organization being referenced here. Certainly one can speak of societies and collectivities as being organic in nature, i.e., of the

zations represent human creations. As such, a given organization is an expression of human culture (Schein, 1985). Reflected in its structure are explicit and/or implicit beliefs, values, goals, and assumptions which facilitate or hinder the realization of desired organizational processes and outcomes. Just as the halls in a building direct and define the flow of traffic in the building, so the structure of the organization directs and defines the flow and pattern of human interaction in the organization.

Given the current attempts to increase collaboration within and among schools, several questions deserve further consideration. Among the most important are these: What patterns of interaction and collaboration among educators are defined by the present school structure? What patterns of interaction and collaboration are *facilitated* by this structure? What patterns of human interaction and collaboration are *hindered* by this structure? To gain insight into these important questions, we must pay attention to the role that teaching and learning—the core technology of schools—plays in determining school structure.

RECONSIDERING THE ORGANIZATION'S CORE TECHNOLOGY

Given the functions served by organizational structure, and the role that structure plays in defining the nature and extent of collaborative efforts, questions regarding its determinants are important to researchers and practitioners. While other factors have been identified as key determinants of organizational structure (Scott, 1995, 1992; Scott & Meyer, 1994; Hall, 1991; Ranson, Hinings, & Greenwood, 1980), the role played by an organization's core technology is of particular concern. Though the precise nature of its influence on structure is debated, an organization's core technology plays an indispensable role in determining the range of structural alternatives available to organizational leaders. Hence, a fundamental understanding of the relationship between technology and structure is essential (Thompson, 1967) for conceptualizing both the possibilities *and* limitations of collaborative efforts within and among organizations.

The word *technology* has traditionally been associated with the tools and hardware used in the production process. Definitions of this nature, however, are excessively limiting. Absent are references to the cognitive processes and skills required to use these implements. Hulin &

---

natural tendency of humans to associate and collaborate. This discussion regarding the artificial nature of organizations is strictly in the context of formal organizations.

Roznowski (1985, p. 47) provide a more comprehensive definition of technology as the physical hardware *and* the methods or intellectual know-how used in the production process.

In an organizational context, core technology may be defined as that set of methods, intellectual processes, and hardware used by the organization and its members to fulfill the organization's primary mission or objective. Although any single organization may engage in many activities using multiple technologies, there is usually one predominant or core activity performed by the organization that defines it as an organization. The primary and predominant activity of public schools is an activity designed to address the important goal of student learning, namely, teaching. Although schools engage in multiple activities using multiple technologies, it is this core activity that defines the school as an organization.

Identification of its core activity and of the technology associated with it is fundamental to understanding the relationship shared between the organization's structure and its technology (Thompson, 1967). Ideally, the structure of an organization should be built around the core activity of the organization and the technology associated with it; that is to say, *form should follow function*. Ideally, the technology associated with the core activity is characterized by a high degree of *technological clarity*. That is to say, this technology is clearly understood by organizational leaders: its individual components are known, the intellectual know-how associated with the most effective use and configuration of these components are known, and a high degree of control can be exercised over them. Ideally, such knowledge is reflected in an organizational structure which allows for the free exercise of this technology. These principles represent ideal states to maximize organizational effectiveness and efficiency.

The following normative propositions capture the essence of these principles as applied to the organizational structure of schools. In order for teachers to be effective in the task of teaching, the structure of the school organization must: (1) reflect the essential components of the technology of effective teaching, be they adequate physical facilities, instructional materials, specific pedagogy, and so forth; and (2) be patterned to allow teachers the freedom to fully engage in the technology associated with the teaching act, that is, the school should be structured and the work of the teaching should be designed in such a way so as to allow teachers to fully engage in those activities associated with effective teaching. For advocates of restructuring, those structural features which both facilitate and hinder this engagement should be identified and considered when planning change.

In reality however, schools, like all organizations, vary in the degree to which their structures satisfy these conditions. For example, schools vary in the degree to which their structures are aligned with the teaching and learning technologies that define them. They vary in the degree to which their structural configurations allow for the free exercise of these technologies. Furthermore, schools vary in the degree to which the teaching technologies that define them are understood.

Consider, as an example of this variability, two types of organizations: the furniture manufacturer and the public school. The core technology of the former has as its focus the manufacturing of dining room furniture, while the core technology of the latter focuses on the process of teaching and learning. The technology associated with furniture manufacturing is fairly clear. The inputs (materials such as wood, metal, etc.) are known and their quality predictable. Likewise, the outcomes (finished dining room tables, chairs, etc.) are known, and the intellectual know-how and processes (e.g., building and finishing methods) required to transform inputs into outputs can be articulated with clarity. Conditions of high certainty such as these allow organizational leaders to structure the organization in such a way as to maximize its effectiveness and efficiency.* In addition, these conditions allow leaders to predict the amount of coordination and collaboration required to complete the task successfully. (Whether organizational leaders actually seek to maximize this alignment, however, is a matter of strategic choice and implementation fidelity.)

In contrast, the core technology associated with public schools—teaching and learning—is characterized by a greater degree of ambiguity (Rowan, 1990; Cohen, March, & Olsen, 1972). The quality of inputs are not uniform or standardized. Students in a classroom do not come to the teacher with equal abilities, the same knowledge base, or identical backgrounds (Moore-Johnson, 1990). The goals of the organization are more diffuse, and the technology associated with the teaching process much more equivocal. What works (e.g., teaching methods and materials) with one student cannot be assumed to work with another. One teacher may have success with a student, while another—using similar techniques and methods—is unsuccessful. As a result, the structure of the organization must reflect and allow for this ambiguity (Weick, 1979; Thompson, 1967). The school must be structured to allow for the needed flexibility to deal with the ambiguity and equivocality associated with the teaching process. Furthermore, given the levels of ambiguity

---

* In making this statement, the ambiguities surrounding attempts to define concepts such as 'organizational effectiveness' and 'organizational efficiency' are recognized. Reading through the literature, one will find multiple definitions of each.

and equivocality associated with teaching and learning, the structure of the school must allow for greater degrees of communication and collaboration among workers at the core. As Thompson (1967) and Weick (1979) note, tasks characterized by higher levels of ambiguity increase the need for communication, collaboration, and the free exchange of ideas among workers.

STRUCTURE, CORE TECHNOLOGY, AND COLLABORATION IN SCHOOLS

Hence, it is argued here that efforts to restructure the school for increased collaboration should begin with a *reconsideration* of these two basic features of the school organization: organizational structure *and* core technology. Advocates of restructuring must think in terms of organizational form, organizational function, and the relationship between the two. *Form* in this context is used in reference to structure; *function* is used broadly to refer to the core technology of the school organization—the teaching-learning process. The following questions seek to relate form and function, and they hint at the kinds of issues which must be addressed when considering attempts to restructure schools:

- What structural features of the school organization (form) promote the effective and efficient exercise of the teaching and learning process (function)?
- What structural features (form) promote the collaborative interactions sought (function)?

In the specific context of restructuring for increased collaboration, these questions may be combined and restated as follows:

- What structural features of the school organization (form) facilitate *or* hinder the collaborative efforts that are needed (function A) to successfully engage in the teaching-learning process (function B)?

PROMISES AND PITFALLS

By juxtaposing these two concepts, form and function, the reflective practitioner gains a framework for thinking about the potential promises and pitfalls associated with increased collaboration in the public school organization. By framing restructuring efforts in this manner, the importance of the teaching-learning process in the public school organization is likewise given primary emphasis. Would-be reformers must consider the effects of a given reform proposal on this defining core activity of schools. Will the proposed change enhance or hinder the teaching-learning process?

To be sure, this can be a very difficult question to answer. The equivocal nature of the teaching-learning process coupled with the complex array of interrelationships and interactions that define the public school organization make such predictions highly uncertain. Nevertheless, given the importance of the teaching-learning process to public education, it is argued here that any and all proposals for restructuring should begin with a consideration of this all important question.

To say that the answer to this question may be difficult in coming, however, is not to say that a measure of insight into the possibilities of a given restructuring proposal cannot be generated a priori. To the contrary, an awareness of a handful of features relating to the social structure of schools provides a useful point of departure for considering the possibilities of a proposed structural change (Johnson & Licata, 1995). While the four features discussed below are not to be taken as an exhaustive rehearsal of the structural features of the school as a social system, they do provide an analytical means for speculating on the possible difficulties, successes, and/or failures that a proposed change will encounter once implementation has begun. When considering attempts to restructure schools for increased collaboration, prominent features such as these be must be considered. Restructuring efforts must be negotiated within the context of these defining structural features.

The first feature to be considered is the nature and character of the work environment which exists in schools (see also Evans-Stout, chap. 7, this text). In the day-to-day life of schools, teachers and administrators find themselves subject to numerous, short, multiple interactions with a variety of individuals. Time is a scarce resource, paperwork is abundant, and frustration is often at or near the threshold level. In sum, school employees find themselves working in what has been identified as a *"stimulus overload," labor-intensive environment* (Willower, 1982, 1973). When considering a proposed change to increase collaboration among teachers or other school participants, will the hindrance or work level of these individuals also be increased? That is, will it require more time, effort, or paperwork on the part of teachers and administrators? Unless this work-level issue is addressed, proposed changes that function to increase the hindrance level of educators will, in the long run, meet with resistance. If, for example, English teachers in a large comprehensive high school are called upon to collectively engage in an extensive revision and alignment of all course offerings in the department, and release time is not allocated for this, that is, teachers are not released from other pressing responsibilities, then the chances of realizing an authentic collaborative effort are greatly diminished.

It should be likewise noted that the organizational demands of increased collaboration create potentially high start-up costs (Johnson & Galvin, 1997; see also Galvin, chap. 4, and Evans-Stout, chap. 7, this text). Such costs are reflected in increased demands upon the communication and coordination systems of the organization. Further, the amount of energy required to increase communication and coordination efforts is directly proportional to the level of collaboration being sought (Scott, 1992). Initial calls for greater collaboration within and between schools may be met with some excitement, but the demands associated with such efforts, once implemented, may lead to increased resistance from organizational members unless the school can be restructured to address such costs. For example, in many schools, teaching assignments and schedules are structured so as to deny teachers the time needed to communicate and coordinate their work. Because work coordination takes more time and effort, teachers and others need to be given regular meeting times during their school day to communicate with one another (see also Pounder, chap. 5, this text). Technology provides one possible solution to this dilemma. Communication networking tools such as electronic mail may be installed to allow for easier, less time-consuming interaction. This presents policymakers with a fundamental challenge. Will this time represent an *added demand* on teachers *or* will provisions be made to reduce demands in other areas so that time can be given to collaborative efforts? In sum, will teachers be freed from other obligations to provide the time for authentic collaboration with others?

A second structural feature which must be considered when planning change in the school organization is *the autonomy norm which defines the teaching profession*. Rooted in the uncertainty surrounding the teaching-learning process and the subsequent flexibility needed to address the varying needs of individual students, autonomy is a value and norm historically associated with the teaching profession and the public school organization (Lortie, 1975; Jackson, 1968; Thompson, 1967; Barnard, 1938). Although autonomy may vary considerably within and among schools (Corwin & Borman, 1988), teachers tend to jealously guard the boundaries of their classrooms from the encroachment of others, be they parents, fellow teaching colleagues, or administrators. Further, within secondary schools in particular, teachers belong to and guard jealously their distinctive subject-based subcultures, each characterized by differing beliefs, norms, and practices (Grossman & Stodolsky, 1995). Radical site-based governance structures with expanded decision-making authority provide an example of how this autonomy can be threatened, particularly when such councils make binding decisions on instructional and classroom-related issues. It should be noted that teachers are but one of many groups represented in the decision-making process. As a result, the educator community may feel that its professional decision-making prerogatives in these areas have been usurped.

Jackson (1968) notes that the autonomy enjoyed by teachers in the classroom is under constant threat from a variety of sources. Advocates for increased collaboration in schools would do well to consider the potential threats of increased collaboration to teacher autonomy. Will attempts to increase collaboration threaten this strong professional norm? Because collaboration involves a trade-off or balancing of individual and group needs (Weick, 1979; Simon, 1981, 1976; Barnard, 1938), will the demands created by increased collaboration require teachers to give up critical levels of individual autonomy? If so, do participants gain group-level autonomy instead? For instance, as Pounder notes in chapter 5 of this text, teamed secondary teachers often find that they have greater autonomy and flexibility in scheduling student instructional time than do individual teachers working under traditional class schedules. These trade-offs must be considered and addressed if collaboration efforts are going to be successful. If collaboration requires teachers or other school participants to compromise on some strong professional norms (such as autonomy), the school structure must be modified to balance these compromises with instructional or professional benefits that educators value as strongly.

Closely aligned with teacher autonomy is *the theme of pupil control.* As noted elsewhere, a prominent feature of the school organization is the degree to which it is structured to control the flow and movement of the students (Willower & Jones, 1973; Willower, Eidell, & Hoy, 1967). Several factors appear to account for this defining feature. As organizations characterized by a high degree of population density, schools coordinate and control student behavior to a high degree. This population density, and the problems created by it, are typically addressed through a variety of crowd-control routines and procedures, for example, strict policies regarding out-of-class behavior, playground activities, student assemblies, and so forth. Attempts to coordinate and control are further complicated by the unselected and captive nature of students. Because public education is compulsory, a certain percentage of students attends school unwillingly. Much as in prisons and other types of "total institutions" (Carlson, 1964; Goffman, 1962), the unselected and captive nature of students create client-control challenges and an underlying adversarial culture between teachers and some students (Waller, 1932).

Such conditions have contributed to the emergence of a strong norm in schools regarding the importance of maintaining order and control.

Perceptions regarding the effectiveness of a given teacher are often tied to his/her ability to maintain order and control in the classroom (Johnson, 1992). Given the strength of this norm, the success of a proposed change must be evaluated in terms of how it challenges or threatens the ability of teachers to maintain control. Will increased collaboration among organizational participants enhance or threaten teachers' ability to maintain order in the school and classroom? Again, examples from teacher teams suggest that teachers working collaboratively may have a broader and more powerful effect on student behavior when they coordinate and consistently reinforce behavioral expectations as a team rather than as isolated individuals (see Pounder, chap. 5, this text). However, if successful collaboration is to be achieved, the issue of coordinated pupil control must be understood and addressed in the school restructuring reforms. As Simmons (1985) has noted, the cognitive abilities of students are organized and constrained by the contexts in which they are used. If collaborative efforts reduce the ability of teachers to maintain order, then this contextual constraint will mitigate teaming efforts aimed at increased collaboration among teachers.

A fourth feature of the school organization which provides further insight into the success of proposed collaboration reforms is *the vulnerability of the public school to its environment.* When used to describe education, the adjective *public* is quite significant (Johnson, 1995). As public institutions supported by tax dollars, schools are accountable to the public and are vulnerable to the demands, supports, and influences of the environment. Not only does the public have a right to raise questions and concerns about schools, but the majority of citizens are themselves products of the public school system. As products of this system, many citizens have definite ideas about what constitutes *effective* schools and teaching. Although the substance of these ideas may vary, this common experience places schools in an unusual position. Unlike organizations such as hospitals, high-tech engineering firms, and Wall Street investment companies which have their own esoteric language, techniques, and modes of operation, schools lack an *organizational mystique.* Having been students themselves, most people know something about how schools operate. These factors highlight the public vulnerability of the school organization.

The public-vulnerability feature of the school organization creates special problems for educators. School personnel find themselves dealing with a number of functional and dysfunctional environmental influences. Of particular importance are those potentially disruptive influences which threaten the ability of the school to successfully perform the core technology which defines it, namely, teaching and learning. As has been noted elsewhere, if workers at the core of an organization are to fully engage in the work, the core itself must be *buffered* from these influences (Ogawa, 1996; Scott, 1992; Thompson, 1967). While it is naive to think that these influences can be totally eliminated, the disruptive effects of these influences on the core technology of the school must be minimized. Hence, restructuring efforts which introduce measures that increase the public vulnerability of the schools, will—over time, if not initially—encounter resistance from organizational participants. Will attempts to increase collaboration among organizational participants increase the public vulnerability of the school? Will such attempts threaten the integrity of those structural features which buffer teachers from the influences of disruptive environmental influences? As noted in a previous example, if school- community councils become a key collaborative problem-solving group, to what degree should these councils address instructional issues such as teaching methods, curriculum and materials choices, grading practices, and so forth? To what degree should decisions about the core technology of schools—teaching and learning—be left to the expertise and domain of school professionals versus lay community people? Which domains of school decision-making should be open to the public and which should not?

It seems reasonable to speculate that attempts to increase *inter*organizational collaboration especially run the risk of increasing this vulnerability. For example, schools collaborating with local businesses and corporations may find themselves somewhat dependent on and vulnerable to the scrutiny of these entities. Financial and/or other types of resources received from these businesses may place contingencies on schools that administrators and teachers find unacceptable. On the other hand, by not accepting these resources, a school may run the risk of garnering negative publicity. In either case, the vulnerability of the school to the public is increased.

These four structural features of the school organization—the stimulus-overload work-environment, the teacher-autonomy norm, the control-orientation structure, and the level of public vulnerability—represent some of factors which must be considered when planning for increased collaboration. Although not intended to be an exhaustive representation of what the school organization is, consideration of these features provides a measure of insight into the potential success of collaborative efforts.

Overcoming these and other barriers may require significant changes for teachers, changes with which teachers may initially struggle. In spite of the ambiguity surrounding the teaching-learning process and the collaborative demands created by it, the historical culture of the teaching profession is such that teachers may find it difficult to look beyond the walls of their own classroom. While teachers may see the need *and* express the willingness for increased collaboration, these features of the school organization suggest a need for assistance in helping teachers direct this willingness toward productive collaborative endeavors. In addition, such structural consideration as the ways in which work is divided among teachers, students are grouped for teaching-learning, and schools are designed should be reexamined. To be sure, restructuring for increased collaboration may represent a formidable challenge, an idea much easier debated than realized. Nevertheless, if increased collaboration is deemed necessary, such restructuring must begin with a fundamental reconsideration of its possible effects on these defining features of the school's social structure.

CONCLUSION

In presenting this framework for conceptualizing discussions of collaborative efforts within and between schools, several ideas are offered for consideration. To begin with, the reader is called upon to *reconsider* two fundamental features of the organization—its structure and core technology. As a human-made artifact, structure plays an important role in defining the patterns of interaction which emerge among organizational participants. Just as the halls in a building define and direct the flow of traffic, so structure functions to define and direct the patterns of human interaction in the organization. In light of demands for increased collaboration, some important questions to ask about the structure of the school organization are these: What patterns of interaction and collaboration are being defined by this structure? What patterns of interaction and collaboration are *facilitated* by this structure? What patterns of interaction and collaboration are hindered by this structure?

On the other hand, the nature of the core technology—the degree to which it is understood and can be predicted—has implications for the *needed* levels of collaboration among organizational participants (Thompson, 1967). Further, an organization's core technology has implications for the *range of structural alternatives* available to leaders. Environmental demands and influences notwithstanding (Scott, 1995; Scott & Meyer, 1994; Meyer & Rowan, 1978), the nature of the organization's core technology sets limits on the structure which emerges to define the organization. This set of observations leads us to consider two additional questions: What levels of collaboration among organizational participants are needed? What levels of collaboration are *possible*? As noted earlier, these questions highlight the importance of seeking a measure of correspondence between structural *form* and organizational *function*. Advocates for increased collaboration in schools should consider this form-function relationship.

This conceptualization offers but one way of framing such efforts. The variability—and at times unpredictable nature—of human behavior in organizations confounds our thinking about the relationships noted above. Nevertheless, consistent with the arguments made by Argyris (1957, 1973), we should think about designing and structuring school organizations in ways that promote the desired patterns of interaction—including collaborative interactions.

REFERENCES

Argyris, C. (1973). Personality and organizational theory revisited. *Administrative Science Quarterly, 18*, 141–167.

Argyris, C. (1957). The individual and organization: Some problems of mutual adjustment. *Administrative Science Quarterly, 2*, 1–24.

Bailyn, B. (1972). *Education in the forming of American society.* New York: Norton.

Barnard, C. I. (1938). *The functions of the executive.* Cambridge, MA: Harvard University Press.

Bellah R. N. (1991). *The good society.* New York: Knopf, Distributed by Random House.

Blau, P., & Schoenherr, R.A. (1971). *The structure of organizations.* New York: Basic Books.

Carlson, R. O. (1964). Environmental constraints and organizational consequences: The public school and its clients. In D. E. Griffiths, *Behavioral Science and Educational Administration* (pp. 262–276). Chicago, IL: University of Chicago Press.

Cohen, M. D., March, J. G., & Olsen, J. P. (1972). A garbage can model of organizational choice. *Administrative Science Quarterly, 17*, 1–25.

Corwin, R., & Borman, K. M. (1988). School as workplace: Structural constraints on administration. In N. J. Boyan, (Ed.), *Handbook of Research on Educational Administration* (pp. 209–237). New York: Longman.

Cuban, L. (1988). A fundamental puzzle of school reform. *Phi Delta Kappan, 69*(5), 341–344.

Dahl, R. A. (1956). *A preface to democratic theory.* Chicago, IL: University of Chicago Press.

Dewey, J. (1916). *Democracy and education.* New York: Macmillan.

Etzioni, A. (1993). *The Spirit of community: Rights, responsibilities, and the communitarian agenda.* New York: Crown.

Goffman, Erving. (1962). *Asylums.* Garden City, NY: Anchor.

Greenberg, E. S. (1975). The consequences of worker participation: A clarification of the theoretical literature. *Social Science Quarterly, 56*, 191–209.

Grossman, P. L., & Stodolsky, S. D. (1995). Content as context: The role of school subjects in secondary school teaching. *Educational Researcher, 24*(8), 5–11.

Hall, R. H. (1991). *Organizations: Structure, process, and outcomes.* Englewood Cliffs, NJ: Prentice-Hall.

Hulin, C. L., & Roznowski, M. (1985). Organizational technologies: Effects on organizations characteristics and individuals responses. In L. L. Cummings & B. M. Staw (Eds.), *Research in organizational behavior* (Vol. 7, pp. 39–85). Greenwich, CT: JAI Press.

Jackson, P. W. (1968). *Life in classrooms.* New York: Holt, Rinehart, & Winston.

Johnson, B. L., Jr. (in press). Resource dependence theory: A political economy model of organizations. In J. Shafritz (Ed.), *International encyclopedia of public policy and administration.* New York: Holt.

Johnson, B. L., Jr. (1995, April). *Principals and the political economy of environmental enactment.* Paper presented at the annual meeting of the American Educational Research Association, San Francisco.

Johnson, B. L., Jr. (1992). *Negotiated meanings of effective teaching: Diverse and competing task conceptions.* Paper presented at the annual meeting of the University Council for Educational Administration, Minneapolis, MN.

Johnson, B. L., Jr. (1990). The logic of restructuring and reform: A conceptual analysis. *Journal of Thought, 25,*(3–4), 67–92.

Johnson, B. L., Jr. & Ellett, C. D. (1997). "Reframing conceptions of school effectiveness in reform: The role of centralization and work alienation." Manuscript submitted for publication.

Johnson, B. L., Jr., & Galvin, P. F. (1997). Conceptualizing school collaboratives and inter-organizational relationships: A consideration of the public choice and organizational economics frameworks. In P. A. Cordeiro (Ed.), *Boundary crossings: Educational partnerships and school leadership* (pp. 99–113). San Francisco: Jossey-Bass.

Johnson, B. L., Jr., & Licata, J. W. (1995). School principal succession and teachers on successor effectiveness. *Journal of School Leadership, 5,* 394–417.

Kingdon, J. W. (1984). *Agendas, alternatives, and public policies.* New York: HarperCollins.

Lortie. D. C. (1975). *Schoolteacher: A sociological study.* Chicago, IL: University of Chicago Press.

Malen, B., Ogawa, R., & Kranz J. (1990). What do we know about school-based management? A case study of the literature. In W. H. Clune & J. H. Witte (Eds.), *Choice and Control in American Education: Vol. 2. The Practice of Choice: Decentralization and School Restructuring* (pp. 289–342). New York: Falmer Press.

Meyer, J. W., & Rowan, B. (1978). The structure of educational organizations. In M. Meyer et al. (Eds.), Environments and Organizations. San Francisco: Jossey-Bass.

Mintzberg, H. (1979). *The Structure of organizations.* Englewood Cliffs, NJ: Prentice-Hall.

Moore-Johnson, S. (1990). *Teachers at work: Achieving success in our schools.* New York: Basic Books.

Morgan, G. (1986). *Images of organization.* Newbury Park, CA: Sage.

Ogawa, R. T. (1996). Bridging and buffering relations between parents and schools. *UCEA Review, 27*(2), 2–3, 12–13.

Pounder, D. G. (1997). Teacher teams: Promoting teacher involvement and leadership in secondary schools. *The High School Journal, 80*(2), 117–124.

Ranson, S., Hinings, B., & Greenwood, R. (1980). The structuring of organizational structures. *Administrative Science Quarterly, 25,* 1–17.

Rowan, B. (1990). Applying conceptions of teaching to organizational reform. In R. F. Elmore (Ed.), *Restructuring schools: The next generation of educational reform.* (pp. 31–58). San Francisco: Jossey-Bass.

Schein, E. H. (1985). *Organizational culture and leadership.* San Francisco: Jossey-Bass.

Scott, W. R. (1995). *Institutions and organizations.* Thousand Oaks, CA: Sage.

Scott, W. R. (1992). *Organizations: Rational, natural, and open systems* (3rd ed.). Englewood Cliffs, NJ: Prentice-Hall.

Scott, W. R., & Meyer, J. W. (Eds). (1994). *Institutional environments and organizations: Structural complexity and individualism.* Thousand Oaks, CA: Sage.

Simmons, W. (1985). Social class and ethnic differences in cognition: A cultural practice perspective. In S. F. Chipman, J. W. Segal, & R. Glaser (Eds.), *Thinking and Learning Skills: Vol. 2. Research and Open Questions* (pp. 519–536). Hillsdale, NJ: Erlbaum.

Simon, H. A. (1976). *Administrative behavior* (3rd ed.). New York: Macmillan.

Simon, H. A. (1981). *The sciences of the artificial* (2nd ed.). Cambridge, MA: MIT Press.

Thompson, J. D. (1967). *Organizations in action.* New York: McGraw-Hill.

Waller, W. (1932). *The sociology of teaching.* New York: Wiley.

Weick, K. (1979). *The social psychology of organizing* (2nd ed.) New York: McGraw-Hill.

Willower, D. J. (1973). Schools, values and educational inquiry. *Educational Administration Quarterly, 9,* 1–18.

Willower, D. J. (1982) "School organizations: Perspectives in juxtaposition. *Educational Administration Quarterly, 18,* 89–110.

Willower, D. J., Eidell, T. L., & Hoy, W. K. (1967). *The school and pupil control ideology.* Monograph No. 24. University Park: Pennsylvania State University.

Willower, D. J., & Jones, R. G. (1973). Control in an educational organization. In J. D. Raths, J. R. Pancella, & J. S. Van Ness & R. G. Jones. (Eds.), *Studying teaching* (pp. 410–416). Englewood Cliffs: Prentice-Hall.

CHAPTER 3

Changing Schools into Collaborative Organizations

James E. Barott and Rebecca Raybould

There is currently a national movement advocating the transformation of schools as they currently exist into more collaborative organizations. The popularity of this movement is evident in a number of literatures and reform movements, as well as the agendas of a number of professional educational organizations. A brief listing of these literatures includes effective schools literature, restructuring literature, leadership literature, supervision literature, and school governance literature, as well as the call for schools to be reframed as communities (Sergiovani, 1994). In addition, a number of professional organizations such as the American Educational Research Association (AERA), the University Council for Educational Administration (UCEA), the National Council of Professors of Educational Administration (NCPEA), and the Association for Supervision and Curriculum Development (ASCD) have used collaboration, community, partnership or closely related concepts as organizing themes for their national conferences in recent years. For example, the theme of the 1995 UCEA conference was "Re-examining Leadership for Community, Diversity and Learning." The 1995 AERA conference was organized around the theme of "Partnerships for a New America in a Global Community." The sessions focused on characteristics of successful partnerships, problems in promoting school and community change, and the new responsibilities that accompany increased interactions between schools, families, and communities. At the national level this movement can be seen in documents such as the 1994 U.S. Department of Education report "Strong Families, Strong Schools," which asserts that a positive correlation exists between children's learning and family involvement.

This suggested transformation or change of school organizations into more collaborative organizations has proven to be a difficult task. Change, when it has occurred at all, has been an expensive, slow, and difficult process. Some school organizations have vehemently resisted this change, and if forced to change they have tended, after a period of time, to return to the way they were originally organized. Schools have a well-known tendency to resist change, and, with the exception of incremental adjustments, many continue to operate much as they have since the turn of the century (see also Evans-Stout, chap. 7, this text). This tendency of schools to maintain the status quo presents a fundamental dilemma for those who wish to transform schools into something they are currently not. That is, in spite of all the good intentions of the experts, schools seem to remain pretty much the same. How can we begin to understand this dilemma and facilitate lasting change?

In this chapter we argue that in order to effectively transform schools into more collaborative organizations we need to change the way we think about organizations, collaboration, and change. We will attend to each of these concepts in turn. We begin with changing the way we think of organizations.

A DEFINITION OF ORGANIZATION

Before we can speak of organizational change, we need to be clear about how we think about organizations. In contrast to taking the structural approach to organizations seen in the previous chapter and in much of the current literature, we advocate a *process* definition of organizing. When we speak of organizing, we are speaking of patterned processes which result from the "relations among parts and relations among relations" (Smith, 1982, p. 318). It is in the patterned processes of the interactions between people that an organization takes its form. From an organizational change perspective, organizational structure is viewed as crystallized processes (Bacharach & Lawler, 1980; Smith 1988). It is because these organizational processes are repeated so often that they appear fixed.

From this perspective, the interactions and relationships between people are not things but processes that take place at interpersonal, group, organizational, and interorganizational levels. A particular pattern of organizing is not a thing one can remold as if it were a piece of clay or redesigned as though it were a machine. This is important, because we make a mistake in our thinking, as well as minimize the opportunity for change, when we reify organizations or think of them as things or nouns (Weick, 1969).

When we speak of changing schools into more collaborative organizations, what we really mean is that we want to change the nature of the relationships, or the patterns of relating. Specifically, we want to change the processes of relating, the rules of the relationships, and the assumptions on which these are based.

COLLABORATION

Interdependence or Autonomy/Discretion

In changing schools into more collaborative organizations, we are asking people to share information, decision making, work together, or *co-labor*. In essence, we are asking them to change the patterns of their relationships so that they are more interdependent. This is in stark contrast to many schools' current relationship patterns, which tend to have an organizational bias in favor of professional isolation, autonomy, or discretion.

This demand for professional discretion—and the belief in it as a primary value—is common to all professions. Professionalism depends, not on compensation or status, but on principles of conduct and governance of an occupation that are client oriented and knowledge based (Darling-Hammond, 1990). Professional discretion arises because professionals need to make judgements about what to do with specific clients. Discretionary latitude is a demand to be allowed to use one's expertise with minimum hindrance from others. This value or ideology is the most generally shared work related norm of school organizations. Teachers demand discretion in their control of the classes, administrators demand discretion in the control of the building, and so on.

As a consequence, many school organizations attempt to buffer their organizational boundaries from outside influences (Ogawa, 1996). For example, principals attempt to maintain parental support while keeping the parents from disrupting the task of the school. Teachers attempt to seal off their classroom from other teachers, parents, and administrators. And, finally, principals and other administrators close governance and decision making processes to teachers, parents, and students.

Increased interdependence often occurs at the expense of professional discretion. Interdependence in any organizational system must be traded off against discretion. Discretion and interdependence are in an either/or relationship. As we stated above, professional discretion is the dominant ideology in the school. It shapes much of the school's behavior through strengthening boundaries against outside influences. However, gains in professional discretion have been won at the cost of decreased public support for education. Collaborative schools are proposed as one solution to this phenomenon of decreased public support. Professional discretion has evolved as a solution to the problem of providing teaching and learning opportunities to clients. These solutions are clearly in conflict. It is important to keep in mind that collaboration and increased interdependence can come only at the cost of professional discretion, and vice versa.

Collaboration and Conflict

As we stated above, opportunities for collaboration arise with the increased interdependency among teachers, administrators, students, parents, and community members. At the same time, with increased interdependency comes the opportunity for conflict. Opportunities for collaboration and conflict arise together from interdependency. Therefore, we can not talk meaningfully about increasing collaboration in school organizations without also attending to conflict. The literature on changing schools into collaborative organizations is filled with descriptions of the positive contribution collaboration makes to successful schools. What is generally not attended to is the potential influence of conflict.

Interdependency creates the potential for conflict because people's intentions, goals, means, and ideologies vary (Pfeffer, 1981). With these differences come the potential for very real and legitimate conflict. One way to minimize this conflict is to privatize it through increased professional discretion and autonomy. One way to increase conflict is to socialize it through increased interdependency (Schattschneider, 1975).

In school organizations the major differences that shape organizational behavior occur at the boundaries between the organization's primary constituent groups: administrators, teachers, students, parents, and the district. Collaborative relationships allow us to take advantage of these differences and use them as strengths in our work. At the same time, these differences can also lead to conflictive relationships in which we fight over the differences.

Those who work toward changing schools into more collaborative organizations must keep in mind that with increased interdependence come increased opportunities for both collaboration and conflict. Successful efforts to change require that organizational members be aware of this dynamic, as well as have the ability to work with both collaboration and conflict. Taking these dynamics into account guards against any utopian fantasies we may have about the benefits of collaboration while denying the costs. This awareness also serves to enhance our efforts at successfully changing schools into more collaborative organizations.

Costs, Benefits, and Scarcity

Interdependent relations (both collaborative and conflictual) provide the opportunity for both benefits and costs to all parties. Costs and benefits include loss of discretion, gains in influence, increased information, time demands, and so on. The distribution of costs and benefits among organizational members is an important element that shapes the nature of school organization. An important question to consider is what will be gained or lost if a particular change in the patterns of relating. That is: Who benefits and who loses?

Schools operate under conditions of scarcity. There is never enough time, attention, money, and so on to go around. Given a choice about how to organize, educators will be attentive to the relative costs of alternative ways of organizing. Our argument is that under conditions of scarcity, the cost of alternative ways of organizing influences which organizational processes are adopted by a school organization as well as which persist over time (Barott & Galvin, in press). It is important to realize that change is achieved and/or persistence is maintained at a cost. Costs and benefits shape and constrain the relationship patterns in schools.

The task of changing the current pattern of relationships in schools also requires that we understand change. Fundamentally, this movement is demanding that we change schools into something that they are *not*. In order for us to understand what this means, we must first understand the concept 'not.' We now turn our attention to the topic of change and the concept of *not*.

CHANGE

"What is" and "What is Not"

In order to think about change, the first thing we have to consider is the dialectic of "what something is" and "what something is not." The movement to change schools into collaborative organizations is fundamentally a demand that we change schools from what they are into something that they are *not*. As Bateson (1972) pointed out, there is really only one way for something to be organized for if it were organized differently, it would be something else (see also Smith, 1982).

Not is at the center of all change. The concept of *not* is complex and presents us with many interesting dilemmas and logical knots (all of which are beyond the scope of this chapter). At the most basic level, *not* is a boundary that summarizes a relationship. This boundary is not a thing: it is a metaphor we use to describe the relationship between entities. In this case we are describing the point of contact between what something is and what it is *not*. For example, Johnny is *not* Susanne or a particular set of relationships in the school is *not* collaborative. It is important to keep in mind that the concept *not* belongs neither to the entity nor to what it is *not* (Smith, 1982, p. 322). That is, when we refer to Johnny as *not* Susanne it is important to keep in mind that we are referring to the relationship between Johnny and Susanne, not simply the individual students. *Not* is a statement at a higher level of abstraction or of a different logical type (Watzlawick, Weakland, & Fisch, 1974; Whitehead & Russell, 1910–13) than either entity. In Bateson's (1972) language, it is a metastatement. It is a rule about how the two entities relate to each other.

As we stated previously, what something is and what it is *not* are in a dialectic relationship. That is, they arise together and define each other. Therefore, what something is and what it is *not* must be considered together. In the case of planned change in schools, we must focus on both how schools are currently organized as well as how we think they should change. When we do this we come face to face with another dialectical relationship which exists between the *persistence* of what is and the movement to *change* something into what it is not. It is to the dialectical relationship between change and persistence that we now turn our attention.

Change and Persistence

Watzlawick et al. (1974, p. 1) noted that "persistence and change need to be explored together in spite of their apparently opposite nature." Whenever we observe a persistent, repetitive chain of events, two questions must arise equally: (1) How does this situation persist? and (2) What is required to change it? This is so because persistence and change are two sides of the same coin, and they arise together. To examine change without consideration of persistence becomes meaningless, as change has no meaning without its opposite, persistence (Brown, 1990). This is because they are in a dialectical relationship. To focus on change without taking persistence into account is like believing that a magnet can exist with only one pole; to understand a magnet you must attend to both north *and* south rather than focusing on north *or* south. The same holds true for change and persistence. This helps us understand Kurt Lewin's famous dictum, "You can not understand a system [how it persists] until you try to change it" (Schein, 1996, p. 34).

We argue that we must think about both change and persistence at the same time in our planned change attempts. We believe that the reason many organizational change attempts in schools fail after brief periods of success is because they attend to only half the picture. That is, when we make either half of this dialectic the single focal point or *figure*, we tend to ignore its opposite. It is this inattention to the total field which dooms most change efforts. It is imperative that we attend both to the forces which act to maintain the system as it currently is and to those forces which are acting to change it into what it is *not*.

Considering both halves of this dialectic provides a more comprehensive map of the total field (Lewin, 1951). Attending to only half of the dialectic leads to either/or thinking. That is, *either* change *or* persistence. This type of thinking sets up a false dichotomy and is counterproductive in our attempt to change schools into more collaborative systems. Another danger in either/or thinking is that it sets up an adversarial relationship which often leads to an impasse in the change process. For example, those who want to change the relationship patterns may define those who want the patterns to persist as resistant. Those who want the patterns to persist may define agents of change as disrespectful, outside agitators, fools, or whatever. There are a number of legitimate reasons for both persistence and change in any social system. One argument in favor of persistence is that the current relationships have proven their utility over a period of time: to change them now could threaten the survival of the system. On the other hand, one of the strongest arguments in favor of change is that current relationship patterns are no longer satisfactory and that unless we change them our survival is endangered. In each case the opposite side of the dialectic becomes something to be defeated or overcome. Those under attack, on both sides, will naturally become more resistant, and a vicious circle is created. That is, more force will lead to more resistance, which leads to more force, which leads to more resistance and so on. In effect, both sides are caught in a battle over survival. Clearly, this is a self-defeating conflict, for to destroy one half of the dialectic is to destroy the system.

In order to understand how to break out of this vicious circle we need to consider and understand that there are two distinct types of change. Each type of change has its own dynamics and calls for its own strategy.

Two Types of Change/Persistence

As we mentioned above, the change literature describes two distinct types or levels of change. These two types of change are found in various intellectual traditions and are given different names in the different traditions. A review of the literature in fields such as biology, communications, learning theory, sociology, and cybernetics reveals the terminology developed to refer to these levels of change (table 3.1).

TABLE 3.1
Levels of Change

Level #1	Level #2
First-order change	Second-order change (Watzlawick et. al., 1974)
First-order cybernetics	Second-order cybernetics (Maruyama, 1963; Mead, 1968; Wiener, 1948; von Foerster, 1979)
Homeostasis	Step-functional change (Ashby, 1952; Jackson, 1959)
Morphostatis	Morphogenesis (Maruyama, 1963)
Single-loop learning	Double-loop learning (Argyris, 1976; Argyris & Schon, 1978)
Learning I	Learning II, (Bateson, 1972)
Homeostasis	Dissipative Structures (Perls, 1973; Prigonine, 1978)
Quantitative	Qualitative (Marx, 1976; Hegel, 1929)
Stabilization	Transformation (Fullen, 1993; Quartz, 1995)

Whatever name they are given, these two types of change differentiate between: (1) change *within* a system of organizing that allows the basic nature of the system to persist and (2) qualitative change in the basic nature *of* the system of organizing itself. In the following discussion we will use the concepts of first-order change and second-order change in order to avoid confusion for the reader.

As we mentioned above, first-order change is change within a system of organizing which allows the basic nature of the system to persist. This level is "adjustive, quantitative, and a change of variables" within the system of organizing (Merry & Brown, 1987, p. 99). Examples of adjustive change in schools include the following:

1. One class of students graduate in the spring and a new class enters in the fall.

2. Three teachers retire, one teacher returns to graduate school to obtain an administrative credential, one teacher is fired, and two teachers move to new schools. Seven appropriately credentialed teachers are hired to replace those that departed.

3. The president of the PTA steps down after her term expires and is replace by a new president the next year.

In each of the above examples, the changes are clearly adjustive. Parts of the system are replaced while the basic nature of the system of organizing persists.

As we mentioned above, first-order change can also be quantitative. That is, the number of components within the system of organizing may be increased or decreased without altering how these components inter-relate. For example, the school-age population of a district may increase. In order to accommodate this change, new teachers will be hired. In this way, the basic nature of the school persists. Specifically, the patterns of relationships within the school as well as between the school and it enrollment area remains the same. As these examples illustrate, in first-order change, the more things change the more they stay the same.

Second-order change is qualitatively different from first-order change. In second-order change the basic nature of a system of organizing changes. That is, the social system's relationship patterns change. Second-order change is a change in the rules about how components of a system relate with one another. (Recall our definition of organizing as a patterned process of relations.) By extension, second-order change is also a change in the underlying assumptions about how the components of a system should relate to one another. Examples of second-order change in schools include the following:

1. A teacher changes from a lecture format to cooperative learning in her classroom
2. A group of teachers change from individual instruction to team teaching
3. The decision making system of the school changes from autocratic to democratic
4. The governance system of the school changes from bureaucratic to school/parent councils

In each of the examples cited above the relationship patterns, rules, and underlying assumptions have changed. In the first example, students are no longer required to spend the entire class period in their seats but are required to spend some time working in teams with other students. This is a fundamental shift in the nature of the relationships among students. This example also illustrates a change in the nature of the relationship between the teacher and her class. Accompanying this change is a shift in underlying assumptions. It is a shift away from individualism and teacher as expert to community and student as expert. The change is thus open to challenge on both grounds. The second example illustrates a change in the rules of relating among teachers. The third example illustrates a change in the rules of decision making between teachers and administrators. And finally, the fourth example illustrates a change in the rules of governing between parents and the school. Obviously, each change also represents a change in underlying assumptions. In the last example the change in assumptions is from apolitical schools and administrator-neutral competency to schools as political units and the legitimation of parental influence.

When these examples are taken as a group, it becomes clear that it is possible to have second-order change at one level and persistence at another level. In the first example, change in the classroom does not mean that there will be change in the relationships among teachers, between teachers and the administration, or between parents and the school. In the fourth example, it is possible to have a second-order change in the governance relationship between parents and the school and no change in the classroom or among any of the school's other component groups.

To summarize, it is essential that when we plan for change in school organizations we are clear about whether it is first-order or second-order change we wish to achieve, as well as about the organization level on which we wish to achieve it. The level defines the target of change, while each kind of change calls for its own particular strategy. Many failures in organizational change occur because people attempt first-order change when second-order change is called for or vice versa. Another common cause of failure is that those who attempt change fail to specify the organizational level on which they want the change. Or if they do specify the level on which they want the change, they target a different level with the mistaken notion that change on one level will produce change on another.

The other common mistake agents of change make is to confuse problems, difficulties, and impasses. With the groundwork now laid, we turn our attention in the next section to these concepts, as well as to the more strategic topic of how to think about implementing planned change in school organizations.

PROBLEMS, DIFFICULTIES, AND IMPASSES

It is important for the success of any planned change effort that we differentiate among *first-order problems, difficulties, impasses*, and *second-order problems*. We will deal with each of these concepts in turn. When we speak of *first-order problems* we refer to "an undesirable state of affairs which . . . can be resolved through some common-sense action for which no special problem solving skills are necessary" (Watzlawick et al., 1974, pp. 38–39). First-order problems call for first-order change strategies. These strategies are usually instigated in response to deviance from some norm within the system. The deviation from the norm is generally returned to a steady state through the application of its opposite. If the application of the opposite does not produce the desired result, "more of the same" eventually will (Watzlawick et al., 1974, p. 31). As we stated earlier, first-order change strategies resolve first-order problems without altering the structure of the system. This strategy for implementing change serves us well when dealing with many of the problems we encounter in schools. For example, in the illustrations we used earlier, we hire new teachers to replace the ones who have left, we replace the graduating class with an incoming class, and so on.

When we speak of *difficulties* we refer to "an undesirable but usually quite common life situation for which there exists no known solution and which—at least for the time being—must simply be lived with" (Watzlawick et al., 1974, pp. 38–39). Difficulties occur when we encounter differences for which there are no solutions. Some common examples of difficulties encountered in schools include gender differences, role differences, status differences, ethnic differences, age differences, and so on. A difficulty is a situation that cannot be changed. Since it has no solution, we must simply live with it, accepting the differences. This is obviously the recommended strategy for dealing with differences. However, we sometimes mishandle difficulties. There are two common ways in which we can mishandle difficulties. We will discuss each in turn.

The first way to mishandle a difficulty is to deny that a difference or difficulty exists. For example, one difficulty school organizations face is the difference between the role expectations of parents and teachers concerning the children under their care. Parents want what is best for their own children. Teachers, who are responsible for an entire class of children, must give priority to the interests of the group. This difference in role expectations creates difficulties, as every parent and teacher can attest. This is the basic tension between the few and the many. If this difference is denied by either party, it can lead to an *impasse* between the parents and teacher. Impasses set up an adversarial relationship between the two parties and precludes change. An impasse is created and maintained through the mishandling of difficulties.

A second way that difficulties are mishandled is by trying to change an unchangeable difficulty. In the attempt to solve difficulties, an impasse is created by insisting a solution exists when there is none. This is utopian thinking. For example, it is utopian to assume that the inherent difficulties in schools will be solved through collaboration, or inclusion, or site-based management, and so on. It is naive to imagine that any of these solutions will resolve the difficulties inherent in the organizing of schools. In addition, unrealistic expectations set people up for failure. Any of these solutions taken to extreme becomes a prescription for disaster. Taken to extremes, they are guaranteed to produce an impasse and, hence, no change.

When people attempt to solve a difficulty, they mistakenly frame difficulties as first-order problems and apply first-order change strategies. In this way an impasse is created. For example, a common difficulty encountered by teachers in the classroom is the demand by students for individual attention in a group setting. In some cases students may engage in behaviors which draw attention to themselves and at the same time disrupt the classroom. Teachers often attempt to change the student's behavior by applying sanctions of some sort. This may lead the student to act out again, which leads to greater attempts to control by the teacher, and so on. In this way a game without end is created (Watzlawick, Beaven, & Jackson, 1967). In this example, the parties attempt to solve a difficulty using first-order change strategies. Under this circumstance an impasse arises as a consequence of "the result of wrong attempts at changing an existing difficulty" (Watzlawick et al., 1974, p. 36). First-order change strategies can create impasses when they are applied to difficulties.

Impasses are points of "stuckness" which by their nature preclude change and guarantee persistence. Often we simply live with impasses. However, if more of the same is continually applied to the impasse, the solution (either denial of the difficulty or trying to solve a difficulty) may become a *second-order problem*. The difference between an impasse and a second-order problem is one of degree. Second-order problems are situations in which continued attempts at more of the same lead to a situation which escalates. This escalation results in a qualitative shift in which discomfort increases, and a number of unanticipated consequences result. When this occurs, it is the solution itself which becomes the problem which must be addressed and changed. In our previous example, if the attention-getting behavior of the student and the controlling behavior of the teacher continue to escalate, a point will be reached at which both parties become increasingly miserable and the rest of class suffers.

Second-order problems exist when the solution has itself become the problem. Second-order problems require second-order change strategies. As we mentioned earlier, second-order change strategies address the rules and underlying assumptions on which the patterns of relating are based. To resolve second-order problems requires that we change the rules and underlying assumptions. For example, in the illustration cited above, what is needed is less control by the teacher and less attention-seeking behavior by the student. In order to solve this second-order problem, the student must give up seeking attention in order to get it and the teacher must give up control in order to get it. Second-order change strategies appear paradoxical from a first-order change perspective. However, by becoming aware of the rules and assumptions that are holding the current relationship in place, it is possible to change them and thus resolve second-order problems. What cannot be changed are the underlying difficulties.

PROMISES AND PITFALLS IN CHANGING SCHOOLS INTO COLLABORATIVE ORGANIZATIONS

A number of difficulties are built into the organization of schools and are essentially unresolvable. The current relationship patterns and underlying assumptions in schools have arisen as solutions to these inherent difficulties. For example, from a cultural perspective these patterns are solutions to the difficulties of internal integration and external adaption (Schein, 1990). Relationship patterns also form to handle the difficulties inherent in information processing and decision making (Galbraith, 1973; March & Simon, 1958). Organizational relationship patterns are also solutions to political contests (Pfeffer, 1981), as well as solutions to the difficulties created by complexity and uncertainty of the school's task and environment (Lawrence & Lorsch, 1967; Thompson, 1967; Woodward, 1965). From an economic perspective, these patterns arise as organizations attempt to solve the difficulties of agency (Barney & Ouchi, 1986) and transaction costs (Williamson, 1986). We could go on, but we will stop here as we believe the preceding examples amply illustrate our point.

If people choose to change schools into social systems that are more collaborative in their patterns of relating, it is important to acknowledge and be prepared for the fact that there will be both costs and benefits to the parties involved. There is no free lunch, no utopian solution, no simple resolution. Paradoxically, it is our attempt to solve these difficulties that leads to some of our largest problems.

As we stated earlier, attempting to solve difficulties often leads to impasses which act to preclude change and promote persistence. What has happened in schools is that these impasses are now leading to second-order problems as the solutions have become the problem. For example, solving the difficulties that exist between the role expectations of professional educators and parents by keeping parents out of the schools has escalated to a second-order problem with the unanticipated consequence of decreased community support for schools.

Collaboration is a second-order solution to a second-order problem. It is vital that reformers realize that the previous solutions in schools, while costly, have worked to handle a number of difficulties over a period of time. It is important to stress that these solutions did not solve the underlying difficulties and have created impasses and, hence, persistence. Collaboration will not and can not solve these difficulties. These are simply part of life in schools and must be lived with. However, the change process will bring these difficulties out into the open. If these difficulties can be accepted as part of life, the possibility for change is enhanced. If these differences are denied or utopian solutions are imposed, schools will again become stuck in impasses which will lead to new second-order problems.

For these reasons, changing schools is inherently dangerous, and the potential for the escalation of conflict is always present. We are simply not that good at accepting differences. The push for conformity and the desire of some to control is simply too great, as is the tendency to label those who disagree as "bad." These behaviors preclude change and result in more of the same. The promise is that by acknowledging the difficulties inherent in collaborative relationships we have the opportunity to use our differences as strengths and not waste our time and energy on hopeless solutions to unresolvable difficulties. In this way, we open up the opportunity to devote more of our attention to the education of children.

REFERENCES

Argyris, C. (1976). *Increasing leadership effectiveness*. Malabar, FL: Kreiger.

Argyris, C., & Schon, D. A. (1978). *Organizational learning: A theory of action perspective*. Reading, MA: Addison-Wesley.

Ashby, W. R. (1952). *Design for a brain*. New York: Wiley.

Bacharach, S. B., & Lawler, E. J. (1980). *Power and politics in organizations*. San Francisco: Jossey-Bass.

Barney, J., & Ouchi, W. G. (1986). *Organizational economics: Toward a new paradigm for understanding and studying organizations*. San Francisco: Jossey-Bass.

Barott, J. E., & Galvin, P. F. (in press). The politics of supervision. In G. R. Firth and E. F. Pajak (Eds.), *Handbook of research on school supervision*. New York: Macmillan.

Bateson, G. (1972). *Steps to an ecology of mind*. New York: Ballantine Books.

Brown, G. I. (1990). Toward a methodology for nonviolence. In V. K. Kool (Ed.), *Perspectives on nonviolence* (pp. 97–103). New York: Springer-Verlag.

Darling-Hammond, L. (1990). Teacher professionalism: Why and how? In A. Lieberman (Ed.), *Schools as collaborative cultures: Creating the future now* (pp. 25–50). New York: Falmer Press.

Foerster, H. von. (1979). Cybernetics of cybernetics. In K. Krippendorff (Ed.), *Communication and control in society* (pp. 5–8). New York: Gordon and Breach.

Fullan, M. (1993). Innovation, reform, and restructuring strategies. In G. Cawelti (Ed.), *Challenges and achievements of American education: 1993 yearbook of the Association for Supervision and Curriculum Development* (pp. 116–133). Alexandria, VA: Association for Supervision and Curriculum Development.

Galbraith, J. (1973). *Designing complex organizations*. Reading, MA: Addison-Wesley.

Hegel, G. W. F. (1929). *Science of logic*. London.

Jackson, D. D. (1959). Family interaction, family homeostasis, and some implications for conjoint family psychotherapy. In J. Masserman (Ed.), *Individual and familial dynamics* (pp. 122–41). New York: Grune and Stratton.

Lawrence, P. R., & Lorsch, J. W. (1967). *Organization and environment*. Cambridge, MA: Harvard Graduate School of Business Administration.

Lewin, K. (1951). *Field theory in social science*. New York: Harper and Brothers.

March, J. G., & Simon, H. A. (1958). *Organizations*. New York: Wiley.

Maruyama, M. (1963). The second cybernetics: Deviation amplifying mutual causal processes. *American Scientist, 51*, 164–179.

Marx, K. (1976). *Capital*. Harmondsworth: Penguin.

Mead, M. (1968). Cybernetics of cybernetics. In H. von Foerster, J. D. White, L. J. Peterson, & J. K. Russell (Eds.), *Purposive systems: The first annual symposium of the American Society for Cybernetics* (pp. 1–14). New York: Spartan.

Merry, U. & Brown, G. I. (1987). *The neurotic behavior of organizations*. New York: Gardner Press.

Ogawa, R. T. (1996). Bridging and buffering relations between parents and schools. *UCEA Review*, Vol. 37 (2), 2–3, 12–13. University Park, PA.

Perls, F. (1973). *The gestalt approach and eyewitness to therapy*. Wilmette, IL: Science and Behavior Books.

Pfeffer, J. (1981). *Power in organizations*. Marshfield, MA: Pitman.

Prigonine, I. (1978). Time, structure and fluctuations. *Science, 201*, 777–795.

Quartz, K. H. (1995). Sustaining new educational communities: Toward a new culture of school reform. In J. Oakes & K. H. Quartz (Eds.), *Creating new educational communities* (pp. 240–252). Chicago, IL: University of Chicago Press.

Schattschneider, E. E. (1975). *The semi-sovereign people* (2nd ed.). New York: Holt, Rinehart and Winston.

Schein, E. H. (1990). Organizational culture. *American Psychologist, 45*(2), 109–119.

Schein, E. H. (1996). Kurt Lewin's change theory in field and in the classroom: Notes toward a model of managed learning. *Systems Practice, 9*(1), 27–47.

Sergiovanni, T. J. (1994). Organizations of communities? Changing the metaphor changes the theory. *Educational Administration Quarterly, 30*, 214–226.

Smith, K. K. (1982). Philosophical problems in thinking about organizational change. In P. S. Goodman (Ed.), *Change in Organizations* (pp. 316–374). San Francisco: Jossey-Bass.

Smith, K. K. (1988). Epistemological problems in researching human relationships. In D. N. Berg & K. K. Smith (Eds.), *The self in social inquiry* (pp. 123–141). Newbury Park, CA: Sage.

Thompson, J. D. (1967). *Organizations in action*. New York: McGraw-Hill.

Watzlawick, P., Beavin, J. M., & Jackson, D. D. (1967). *Pragmatics of human communication*. New York: Norton.

Watzlawick, P., Weakland, J., & Fisch, R. (1974). *Change: Principles of problem formation and problem resolution*. New York: Norton.

Weick, K. (1989). *The social psychology of organizing*. Reading, MA: Addison-Wesley.

Weiner, N. (1948). *Cybernetics: Or control and communication in the animal and the machine*. Cambridge, MA: MIT Press.

Whitehead, A. N., & Russell, B. (1910–1913) Principia Mathematica. (2nd ed., 3 vols.). Cambridge, England: Cambridge University Press.

Williamson, O. E. (1986). *Economic organization: Firms, markets and policy control*. New York: New York University Press.

Woodward, J. (1965). *Industrial organization: Theory and practice*. New York: Oxford University Press.

CHAPTER 4

The Organizational Economics of Interagency Collaboration

Patrick F. Galvin

There is an economic character to interagency collaboration that is largely ignored by educational and social service policymakers and program managers. I believe that lack of attention to these economic factors serves as a major obstacle to the development of healthy, strong, and productive collaborations. This chapter will probe and discuss the economics of educational and social service interagency collaborations. First, however, some introductory remarks will help place this current call for reform into an historical context.

THE DELIVERY OF EDUCATIONAL AND
SOCIAL SERVICES: PARALLEL FAILURES

I begin with an observation by Raymond Callahan, author of *Education and the Cult of Efficiency*:

> I am now convinced that very much of what has happened in American education since 1900 can be explained on the basis of the extreme vulnerability of our schoolmen to public criticism and pressure and that this vulnerability is built into our pattern of local support and control . . . Thus it is predictable in 1957 that school administrators would respond quickly to the criticism which followed the launching of the first Russian satellite and would begin to place great emphasis upon science and mathematics . . . the point is not whether more or less science and mathematics should be taught in the schools . . . the point is that when the schools are being criticized, vulnerable school administrators have to respond . . . this pattern of criticism and response has produced some desirable and some undesirable educational changes, but the real point is that this is an inadequate and inappropriate basis for establishing sound educational policy. (1962, p. viii)

Callahan's point seems as applicable to the 1980s and 1990s as it was to the history of education in the first half of this century. During the 1980s, reports like the infamous *A Nation at Risk: The Imperative for Educational Reform* (National Commission on Excellence in Education, 1983), argued that education was failing the needs of Americans and putting the country at risk. Authors like Brimelow (1986) caused a storm of controversy by claiming that society was investing too many of its resources into public and higher education. Brimelow argued that public education was fraught with inefficiency and needed significant reform were it to serve well the economic and social interests of society. Some authors went so far as to argue that the failure of public education was irrevocable; that public education was "dead" (Lieberman, 1993) and would be replaced with privatized educational services. The demands for educational reform were heard from virtually everyone during the 1980s. Just as with the "schoolmen" of Callahan's study, today's school administrators (men and women alike) respond to the criticisms of the day. One of their key responses to the reform demands of the 1980s was to create partnerships with those who criticized them. Thus businesses, those ostensibly threatened by the poor quality of students graduating from schools, were invited into the school to help reform and improve them. Parents, concerned about the quality of schooling for their children, were invited to join with educators to improve education for all. Educators also arranged partnerships with other social service agencies in hopes that such alliances would improve service delivery as well as calm the storm of criticism. Whatever else one can say about these partnerships, it is obvious that any future report whose message resembles that of *A Nation at Risk* will not find school administrators as vulnerable to criticism. Those who have most sternly criticized schools have now had their chance to fix things or at least implement changes: failure need not be born solely by educators.

During this same period of time (1980s), a second crisis was emerging: the failure of America's social service sector. This sector was not castigated with a report comparable to *A Nation at Risk*, but concerns about the efficiency and operation of social service agencies were widespread. The problem was, and still is, frequently sketched out in case studies of situations where children and families "fall through the cracks" in the system, sometimes with disastrous consequences. The problems of these families are often frighteningly complex; the stories tear at the heart of the American dream:

> Charles, a 10th grader, is trying to understand about his own family's turmoil and poverty, violence, and unrest in his neighborhood. An older sister and brother are school dropouts. Another sister recently quit her job as a housekeeper because she could not find safe child care

for her preschooler. His mother was abused as a child and only recently left her husband, who had abused Charles' sisters for years. Even though his mother finished a GED last fall, she has no specific skills and does telemarketing; the family still needs supplemental welfare. As for Charles, he is failing geometry in a class of 50 students. With the exception of carpentry, which he loves, his grades are barely passing. In school, he daydreams frequently, he says, just "wondering what happened." (Melaville & Blank, 1993, p. 5)

The problem, however, doesn't simply revolve around a collection of disturbing case studies; rather, these case studies represent a general condition of society, which seems imperiled. To the families that compose these statistics the reality is stark; to the society that accepts these realities, they wear thin the dream of what we would like to promise our children:

- More than 20 percent of America's children live in poverty; children under six are among the poorest groups in America

- Only about 70 percent of America's students finish high school in four years, and all our efforts to improve that figure have had little effect

- The number of teen pregnancies and teen mothers is steadily rising; births to single teens increased by 14 percent during the 1980s

- Violence among younger people is increasing dramatically; violence is the leading cause of death among teens

- By conservative estimates, at least one hundred thousand children are homeless on any given night (Foundation, 1994; Hodgkinson, 1993; Melaville & Blank, 1993).

Hodgkinson (1993) makes the case that society can not ignore these children and their families. Certainly a sense of moral imperative is one reason, but another is simply economic; if these children fail to grow into productive members of society, then the cost of dealing with the inevitable cycle of poverty, crime, and broken dreams will be huge. Moreover, Hodgkinson notes that the structure of society is changing so that there are fewer and fewer fully employed individuals to support the welfare of retired workers. The failure of our social services to help children like Charles assume a productive role in society is not simply a broken dream for him individually: it threatens the dreams of us all.

These case studies and statistics suggest that the current system of social services does not work well. These failures, according to Melaville and Blank (1993) as well as those at the Annie E. Casey Foundation (1994), are characterized by fundamental and "critical flaws" in the way social services are organized and the way they work:

- Social services are crisis oriented; they are designed to address problems that have already occurred.
- The current social welfare system divides the problems of children and families into rigid and distinct categories that fail to reflect interrelated causes and solutions; problems are administered by dozens of agencies, each funded by different agencies and operating with different guidelines, none of which work well together
- Communication between these various social and education agencies is poor; separate professional training, vocabulary, and purposes keep agencies serving the same audience from working together
- The current system of social services is too specialized and fails to plan, develop, and implement comprehensive services that are needed to deal with the complex problems America's families and children face today (Melaville & Blank, 1993, p. 9; Dunkle, 1993, no. 23)

Demands for change focus on the development of comprehensive programs that are preventative and pro-family in nature—programs that are responsive, convenient, and sensitive to family needs. Efforts to achieve these reforms are focused around promoting integrated, flexible, and responsive organizations. Indeed, Melaville and Blank (1993, p. 15) argue the entire system of social service agencies must be fundamentally restructured such that social service agencies (including education) change the way they think about their work, the way they behave, and the way they use their resources. Collaboration, according to these authors, is the means by which these reforms are achieved. Collaboration requires individuals to change the way they work and use their resources. Further, collaboration is necessary to promote the comprehensive service system desired.

THE HISTORY OF INTERAGENCY
COLLABORATION AS A REFORM POLICY

The call for interagency collaboration during the 1980s and 1990s is not unlike the call for community-schools during the 1960s and 1970s, regional educational service agencies during the 1950s and 1960s, and the original community-schools reform effort during the 1930s.* The

---

* The political values of these reform efforts differ, but all attempt to coordinate in a collaborative framework the various institutional resources within a community to better serve families and children.

community-school movement of the 1930s was an explicit effort to coordinate services and empower the community through interagency collaboration (Ripley, 1939). Schools were viewed as critical to this effort because they were physically close to community members as well as close to the values and concerns of their daily lives.

The 1930s, a decade dominated by what Callahan calls "the cult of efficiency," was a period during which Frederick Taylor and his school of "scientific management" greatly influenced ideas about social organizations. At the core of this movement was the belief that management was capable of and responsible for organizing labor in ways that efficiently produced the services and products desired by society. Organizations, much like biological organisms, were viewed as constantly evolving, with the key to survival being efficiency (Spencer's notion of Social Darwinism). In this view, survival was equated with progress (a severe misreading of Darwin's *Evolution of Species*), and progress was equated with civilization. Thus the promotion of efficient organizations was equated with the evolutionary progress of society.

It is perhaps not surprising that the 1930s was also a period that gave birth to the "human relations" movement, which emphasized the centrality of relationships as key to efficiency and progress—Elton Mayo is frequently cited as the initial leader for this movement (Perrow, 1986). The 1930s were also the time when labor unions were gaining legitimacy and power. Bendix (1956) noted the irony that collaborative management strategies were born during a period of time when the practice of "scientific management" reigned supreme.

During the 1930s, the ideas of efficiency, scientific management, and school district consolidation won out over those of the community school movement, which is now only a footnote to history. The ideas of collaboration were not, however, completely abandoned. Rather, they were incorporated into the ideas of school district consolidation through the proposals for "regional educational service agencies." These agencies were intended to coordinate the activities of multiple schools through collaborative arrangements, so as to gain the efficiencies of scale without abandoning the interests and benefits of local community control. It was an idea that that first took form in 1949 when New York State began funding its Boards of Educational Cooperative Services (BOCES). At that time, New York was the first state to formally organize such cooperatives. A decade later virtually every state in the union would have similarly structured arrangements (Davis, 1976). The success of these agencies were limited, however, and did not lead to the systemic reform of school and community services so widely predicted by proponents of these arrangements.

Elliot L. Richardson, former secretary of health, education, and welfare, is often cited as a leading proponent of the resurgent community-school movement, which became active during the 1960s and 1970s (Gray, 1989; Ringers, 1976). Richardson described the community-school movement as one concerned with the whole person, one concerned with bringing services for people together in a way that makes the most effective use of resources, and one which contributes to a sense of community (Ringers, 1976, p. 23). The community and democratic participation in its operation were key to Richardson's argument for community schools. Interagency collaboration was viewed as a way of creating smaller service units which could operate closer to their clients. Proximity and intimacy of service agencies fostered a sense of belonging, thereby reducing the sense of being a nonentity in a mammoth, bureaucratic social organization.

The value structure underlying the community school movement during the 1960s was one of heightened political awareness and participation. During the 1970s, however, with declining enrollments in schools, high inflation, and a weak economy, the underlying motivation for community schools shifted toward increasing efficiency. The community school was seen as a strategy that would enable social organizations to share space, maximize land and facility use, and minimize the economic burden on the taxpayer while providing integrated multipurpose services to the various groups within the community. Interagency partnerships were thus viewed as a way to more effectively utilize physical as well a human resources. These partnerships resulted from contractual agreements or legislative structures which permitted one agency to work with another. States (e.g., Pennsylvania in 1972), passed legislative acts which allowed cities, counties, towns, schools, and other government agencies to enter into cooperative agreements (Ringers, 1976).

With this involvement of state legislatures, collaborative efforts must be seen as more than initiatives to provide clients with good and useful services that are responsive to their needs; they must be understood in terms of the legal and fiscal environments that constrain their behavior. Societies concerned about how efficiently their resources are being used require a measure of accountability that will add cost and red tape to collaborative partnerships. These costs—that is, the costs of writing contracts and monitoring projects to ensure accountability—detract from the overall viability and potential benefit of collaborative efforts. Costs such as these, so critical to the successful operation of collaborative arrangements, will be further discussed in the chapter's next section.

The interagency reform movement of the 1980s and 1990s looks very similar to reform efforts of past years. Issues of accountability and efficiency still underlie the call for collaboration among social service agencies (Bergquist, Betwee, & Meuel, 1995; Dunkle, 1994; Jones &

Maloy, 1988; Melaville & Blank, 1993; Sarason, Carroll, Maton, Cohen, & Lorentz, 1977). Improving the social condition of people by empowering the community is still a goal of these collaborative efforts (Foundation, 1994). If there is any significant difference, it is in the changed political climate, which views government more suspiciously than in pervious decades.

Individualism and empowerment are seen as alternatives to governmental solutions to community problems. Individuals are seen as the driving force behind the negotiations necessary to develop and sustain collaborative partnerships (Eisenberg, 1995; Gray, 1995; Levine & Trachtman, 1988). These individuals are considered essential for creating and sustaining a climate of cooperation. Thomas Payzant, when discussing the organization of San Diego's New Beginning interagency collaborative, indicates it is essential that a few individuals be willing to constantly keep after the details of project coordination. Without these individuals the collaborative climate, so essential to successful projects, breaks down. Within this perspective on the centrality of individual effort to the success of collaboration, five essential elements of partnership are frequently identified:

1. *Top Level Commitment*: the executive and administrative head of each agency must be dedicated to the success of the project

2. *Defined Goals and Objectives*: an understanding of the goals, written or otherwise, serves as a blue print for the project

3. *Two-way Communication*: easy channels of two-way communication are essential throughout all phases of the partnership

4. *Attitudes*: the "can-do" attitude toward providing services must be adopted by everyone involved; one "bad apple" can spoil the whole effort

5. *Reassessment and Evaluation*: periodic evaluation of the project and procedures under which it operates is essential to retain the vitality of the relationships (Melaville & Blank, 1993; Ringers, 1976)

In essence, forming interagency partnerships or collaboratives is much like forming a business partnership (Alter & Hage, 1993; Ringers, 1976). Each agency brings assets and liabilities to the partnership. While a positive climate for cooperation is an important way of reducing the social friction associated with planning and implementing programs, the justification for investing one's resources into collaborative ventures will depend upon the perceived benefits versus the perceived liabilities (Alter & Hage, 1993; Gray, 1989; Sarason et al., 1977). Obviously there are enormous potential benefits to be gained from collaboration amongst agencies, but there are also enormous potential costs, several of which have been mentioned above. Perhaps this point helps explain the finding that most long standing interagency collaboratives are the result of mandated initiatives rather than voluntary ones (Evan, 1993; Hall, Clark, Giordan, Johnson, & Roekel, 1977). It is an unfortunate reality that the promise of interagency collaboration does not always fully realize its potential.

UNFULFILLED PROMISE

As already noted, schools are frequently cited as good locations for coordinating interagency efforts (Kirst & Kelley, 1995). Around the country, numerous pilot programs have been tested and recognized. The San Diego School District, for example, provided a good illustration of the potential for what is sometimes described as "one-stop coordinated service centers." Working with a variety of social, welfare, and medical services, the superintendent of the San Diego School District, Tom Payzant, has crafted a coordinated program called "New Beginnings." Housed in one of the district's elementary schools, the program reaches out to families and provides a coordinated system of services that is responsive to and supportive of families. The New Beginnings program is one among hundreds being developed and promoted as possible models of collaboration (e.g., A Child's Place program for homeless children in Charlotte, North Carolina; the School of the Future program in Houston, Texas, to name but two).

The assumption underlying the organization of these social/educational collaborative programs, in whatever form, is that they promote effective and useful services to clients, often at a savings to tax payers. The problem is that the evaluation evidence from these programs does not support this claim. Kusserow (1991) examined twenty years of efforts to integrate social and educational services. His report concluded that interagency collaboration frequently results in short term improvements in the accessibility of services for some clients but has little permanent effect on the operation of key institutions. Indeed, as reviewing the literature describing collaborative efforts gives one a clear sense that most collaborative ventures are built upon past failures and an explicit agreement among members to limit rather than expand their efforts (see Levine & Trachtman, 1988; Rigsby, Reynolds, & Wang, 1995; Sarason et al., 1977). In other words, it takes considerable skill and effort to develop a successful collaboration. Tom Payzant recognizes this point when he notes, "collaboration is in vogue and there is a lot of rhetoric, but that can be, as with most things, superficial . . . real change requires dedicated, hard work" (Dunkle, 1994, p. 22).

WHY DOES INTERAGENCY COLLABORATION
NOT SUCCEED MORE OFTEN?

Explanations for the failure of collaborative efforts are many and include issues such as a lack of trust, failure to achieve open communication, protection of one's own "turf," and problems generated by dissimilar training and jargon for professionals from different agencies (Dunkle, 1993, 1994; Gray, 1995; Kusserow, 1991; Sarason et al., 1977). Despite these potential obstacles, proponents of interagency collaboration encourage frontline service agents to continue fighting the good fight for the sake of children and families (Alter & Hage, 1993; Davis, 1976; Gray, 1989; Jones & Maloy, 1988; Levine & Trachtman, 1988; Melaville & Blank, 1993; Ringers, 1976). These proponents argue that with sufficient effort, compromise, and cooperation, the range of possible partnerships is limited only by the ingenuity of those who plan and implement them.

Peter Drucker (1989), an economist and social commentator, notes that reforms are often introduced as an economic matter, which is to say that the reform is believed to operate more effectively and efficiently than the status quo. This is certainly true of the literature about interagency collaboration. Once institutionalized, however, reforms tend to take on a moral quality: the reform becomes an absolute rather than an alternative. It becomes a symbol that is sacred rather than a means to an end. Thus, Drucker notes, the absence of desired outcomes does not raise questions about whether one should do something different. Rather, questions about the effectiveness of collaborative efforts lead to calls for redoubling effort in the name of the good initially invoked.

Economic matters, however, are judged according to a cost/benefit ratio. Economic thinking assumes that choice is based on a calculation of the relative merits of one alternative compared to another, rather than on a philosophical view of the world. Thus, choices about how or whether to organize collaborative services is a matter of comparative value where consideration of costs is central to the judgment. Generally, it is assumed that individuals will avoid costs when possible. Thus, if one holds the quality of some desired service constant, and gives a choice about how to produce that services that differs in cost, it is assumed that the less expensive means of production will be chosen.

THE CHARACTER OF ECONOMIC COSTS

According to Thomas (1971), in his book *The Productive School: A Systems Analysis Approach to Educational Administration*, one of the most important contributions of economic theory to educational administration is the explication of costs and the role of costs in decision making. It is not unusual for most educators to equate costs with expenditures. Costs as expenditures are defined as the monetary outlay associated with the purchase of educational inputs such as teachers, desks, books, facilities, and buses.

Economists describe costs more broadly and include consideration of nonmonetary factors associated with production. These include consideration of professionals' (e.g., teachers, social workers) and administrators' time, expertise, attention, interest, and perhaps even sense of affiliation. Consideration of nonmonetary costs is particularly important when interpreting efforts directed toward the implementation of new ideas in education. The salaries and overhead costs are often fixed, but the indirect and nonmonetary costs associated with how teachers distribute and use their time are not so clearly delimited. If one is to understand the influence of costs on choices over the adaptation of collaborative innovations, then a consideration of the nonmonetary costs as well as direct monetary costs is essential.

COLLABORATION, COSTS, AND DECISION MAKING

The literature about collaboration is full of references to costs, but none of these references are part of a systematic analysis of the role costs play in the organization and delivery of services through interagency arrangements (Alter & Hage, 1993; Crowson & Boyd, 1992; Dunkle, 1995; Gray, 1989; Levine & Trachtman, 1988; Melaville & Blank, 1993; Sarason et al., 1977). Most of these authors acknowledge there are certain costs associated with collaboration, costs much like the "hard work" that Payzant refers to above and the time it takes to implement and maintain collaboration. While these costs are specifically identified, they are frequently portrayed simply as obstacles that must be overcome rather than factors affecting decision making; proactive cost/benefit analysis is conspicuously absent, and costs serve instead as evidence that success will require considerable work. This perspective resembles Drucker's (1989) view of policy as a moral agenda, where evidence of failure simply suggests that one must redouble efforts. Systematically anlyzing costs would allow planners to incorporate findings into a framework to guide their decisions on whether to pursue collaborative arrangements, what kind of projects to form collaboratively, and how these collaborative projects be structured and contracted.

In this section, three types of costs are identified: coordination costs, opportunity costs and information costs. Discussion will be kept relatively brief, as the main purpose is to highlight the nature of costs that are not frequently recognized by proponents of collaboration. There is no intention of portraying individuals as hyperrational economic decision-makers. To the contrary, individuals are explicitly assumed to operate with bounded rather than perfect rationality, great uncertainty, and high risk (March & Simon, 1958). The point is that individuals may value collaboration and all its attendant ideologies and still decide in specific circumstances to forego collaboration and work independently. Such decisions should be viewed not as a failure of the system but rather as evidence of thoughtful decision making. Obviously not all activities need to be organized or delivered collaboratively; the challenge is to identify those that are advantageously organized collaboratively and create an attractive incentive structure that encourages decision makers to consider collaboration.

Coordination Costs

One of the most frequently cited costs associated with collaboration is that associated with the need for communication and planning, or coordination costs. Coordination is the effort required to turn an opportunity into a finished product of some value. The potential collaboration holds for individuals in organizations is the opportunity it creates for them to gain access to new working strategies, new resources, and even new markets (people with whom they work or serve). But the potential of opportunities associated with access to these new resources can be realized only if people follow through and develop plans that coordinate their efforts in ways that positively affect desired outcomes. If the collaboration is formed but subsequently underutilized, the net effect can be to create a more expensive service. Considering the complaint that many social service agencies are overcommitted and underfunded, the potential for new collaborative opportunities to be formed and not used is high. Indeed, several authors described this tendency as "projectitis," where the agencies begin lots of projects but never finish them. Gray (1995) points out that in such cases the cost of coordinating these efforts is more than these agencies can handle or afford, even if the merged or expanded services are desirable and more responsive to the needs of their clients.

Opportunity Costs

As noted, the planning, implementation, and maintenance of collaborative ventures requires people's time, attention, and expertise. While it is true that the commitment of these resources might be more effectively utilized in a collaborative venture, it is also true that the commitment of those resources means some other element of the existing organization (school or social service agency) is not receiving those resources. In this way, collaborative efforts can represent a diversion of resources in organizations that are often financially constrained. Moreover, the commitment of these resources often requires some form of accountability, necessitating expenditure of administrative time that could be used for some other purpose. When people talk about programs requiring hard work in order to succeed, administrators should interpret these phrases as costs to the organization both in terms of obvious direct expenditures and in terms of the less visible costs that represent forgone benefits. An example is the case in which administrators commit resources to some endeavor, only to discover that by doing so they have lost other opportunities that would have proved more beneficial to their purposes and goals. Failure to recognize these costs or assume that reluctance to form collaborative ventures is due to personal attitudes about independence and collaboration is mistaken. In fact, such decisions often prove rational and economically sound.

Information Costs

Present-day school administrators are besieged with criticism of how costly schooling is given the poor outcomes. As Callahan (1962) suggested, it is not surprising that administrators vulnerable to these criticisms will respond by trying to find more efficient ways of producing and delivering educational services. The problem is that without a clear definition of what signifies "quality outcomes" it is very likely that the only guide for administrators will be comparing unit costs. Thus, as has been the case with administrators of past years, the likely direction of these policy initiatives is to produce cheap services rather than to create an efficient system of service delivery (where issues of quality would be explicitly considered in relationship to costs). Understanding the more complex meaning of efficiency and the microeconomics of interagency collaboration is important if administrators are to avoid the crude practice of simply reduing unit costs. Gaining this understanding represents another cost associated with collaborative ventures—information costs.

Obtaining the information needed to faciliate good choices can be costly, especially if the search requires visiting other sites and making judgments based on a systematic analysis of collected data. Program administrators are busy and their time is limited, so often there is not much slack time to undertake a serious analysis of program alternatives. Nonetheless, these information costs, along with the coordination costs and opportunity costs discussed previously, are powerful factors influencing decisions to adopt and implement collaborative programs. The apparent reluctance of individuals to participate in or commit to collaborative ventures may not be solely, or even primarily, due to their attitudes and values. Rather, when the costs of coordinating collaboration are high, or forgone opportunities are great, or information about risky ventures are limited and expensive to obtain, a rational choice may be simply to avoid such arrangements, if the circumstances of the status quo permit it.

OWNERSHIP AND CAPITAL AND ORGANIZATIONAL STRUCTURE

The previous section highlights the potential impact of certain costs on the decisions of individuals considering the involvement of themselves and their organizations in collaborative ventures. An advantage to thinking about collaborative organizations in economic terms is that this exercise organizes what otherwise appears to be an idiosyncratic, circumstantial set of behaviors into a systematic framework from which one can make predictions about choices. Collaboration is described by Melaville and Blank (1993), Dunkle (1994), and many others as a reform movement; it is envisioned as a means for changing the entire system by which educational and social services are produced and delivered. If they are to be successfully implemented, reforms require policies based on a systematic analysis rather than—as Callahan (1962) suggested is more often the case—a cycle of criticism and response. The discipline of economic thinking helps establish such a systematic framework.

An economic perspective can be used to create a more accurate and complete cost/benefit analysis of collaborative ventures. The chapter's final section turns to another set of costs not widely recognized but powerfully influential on the way organizational (and collaborative) arrangements are structured.

Ownership

Ownership refers to a system of agreements about who has the right to decide how resources available within an organizational environment can be utilized. In the simplest example, where one individual brings a million dollars to start up a business, the question of ownership is fairly straightforward. An individual entrepreneur bears the risks and also has the rights to use residual profits (those above operation costs) generated by the business in ways that satisfy his or her interests.

Corporate structure presents a more complicated system of ownership because stocks are sold and there are multiple owners. In these cases, the principals (owners) hire agents (administrators) to manage business. Of course, true owners do not manage daily business operations and hence lack sufficient command of the business details to know whether managers are conducting affairs in ways consistent with their best interests. The uncertainty of these circumstances, and especially the possibility that the managers will opportunistically deceive the owners, creates the need for a system of monitoring that simply was not required by the owner/manager described above.

In those cases in which the outcomes of an organization's effort are easily observed and quantified, this system of monitoring can work relatively easily and efficiently. As the means by which organizations produce outcomes becomes less easily defined and the outcomes themselves are less easily observed and quantified, and require greater qualification to justify, then the cost of monitoring increases. Assuming that organizations, like individuals, are sensitive to these costs there will be a point at which the cost of monitoring outweighs the potential benefits and alternative arrangements will be sought out. When the outputs and processes of production are not easily monitored one possible approach is to control the inputs.

Education and social services are examples of organizations in which the production function is not easily quantified and neither are the outcomes. Moreover, the "owners" are really taxpayers who are represented by government officials at federal, state, and local levels. Funding for these services comes from a myriad of sources because the benefits of these services are broadly distributed across private and public sectors in ways that are extremely difficult to analyze, let alone account for. In these circumstances, monitoring devices are often limited to controlling the inputs through budgetary mandates and program evaluations.

Despite these complications the nature of educational and social service organizations is vastly less complicated than those of interagency collaborations. If issues of ownership are confusing in the current organizational environment that governs educational and social service agencies then imagine the confusion when these two organizational environments attempt to "pool resources to respond to common interests." The problem of monitoring these arrangements becomes even more difficult and complicated because of the increasing number of individuals and agencies who have a need to know, and because of the varying criteria by which they all will judge the effectiveness of program efforts.

Charles Burner (1991), writing for the Education and Human Services Consortium, helps clarify this point by noting that individuals within an organization who are given the authority to use their own discretion, without holding concurrently the accountability of ownership (although he does not use this term), may abuse the system by following courses of action which reflect their own prejudices and biases to the detriment of their clients (p. 24). Within an organizational environment that is clearly defined bureaucratically, one with permanence over time, individuals who are subjected to this abuse have clear lines of recourse. Within a collaborative venture, where lines of bureaucracy and structure are unclear, such accountability is difficult to resolve easily.

Barney and Ouchi (1986) outline a line of research referred to as "organizational economics." The basic theory is that one can explain why organizations structure themselves as they do by examining the costs associated with governing and monitoring. In the simplest of comparisons these authors, referencing the work of Coase (1937) and Williamson (1986), distinguish between those exchanges organized in the marketplace from those conducted within an organizational structure. If one views this contrast as a continuum rather than a dichotomy, then collaboration is a movement toward a more open, free flowing exchange between organizations that resembles the open market place more than self-contained, self-sufficient organizations. Where the cost of monitoring exchanges among ambiguous owners increases, the theory predicts that the tendency will be toward establishing hierarchical organizations where lines of accountability are more easily established. The advantage of hierarchical organizations versus horizontal ones, like that of collaborations, is that the cost of monitoring can be reduced because the flow of information is coordinated within the organization to meet administrative needs. Moving information across organizational domains requires adjustments, in timing, format, and purpose—all of which increase the cost of information flows.

Where *trust* between agencies seeking to establish collaborative ventures is high, the need for monitoring is significantly reduced. Trust is the constant refrain of proponents of collaboration (see Alter & Hage, 1993; Bruner, 1991; Crowson & Boyd, 1992; Gray, 1995; Melaville & Blank, 1993; Sarason et al., 1977). Trust emerges in these discussions as an element critical to the success of collaboration. In Levine and Trachtman's case studies of educational partnerships with businesses, trust is the lubricant that makes collaboration possible. Situations in which individuals or organizations trust one another have little need for monitoring or writing up contingency contracts that assure agreement on who has the right to use resources as they see fit. The analogy of trust as a lubricant is an appropriate one, because the costs of resolving ownership issues can be thought of as friction that drags to a stop the most well intentioned initiatives (Williamson, 1986).

With regard to trust and its impact on monitoring costs, ownership is still the key issue. At the programmatic level, there is the concern about how to monitor frontline workers. Now consider what these general points mean for the de facto owners funding these organizations. Recall that these owners are really the taxpayers, who through representatives they elect pass legislation enabling and funding the operation of education and social service agencies. Funding sources are so distant from the managers hired to administer these programs, particularly as funds trickle down through state and local governmental agencies, that there is little chance of establishing trust in the way proponents of collaboration envision it. Thus, monitoring and associated costs will always be an issue, particularly in the legalistic environment of government whose business it is to account for how it spends taxpayers' money.

Dunkle (1995), writing for The Institute for Educational Leadership (a policy group out of Washington D.C. focusing on interagency collaboration) lays out, in a report entitled, *Who Controls Major Federal Programs for Children and Families: Rube Goldberg Revisited*, a particularly intriguing picture of funding for federal social service programs. As one of its main points, the report asserts that the current system of social services funding presents a tortuous maze through which monies trickle down to state and local governments. Dunkle argues that this system of fragmented funding is driven primarily by the politics of self-serving congressional members and departments that want credit for the passage of bills satisfying special interest groups. Dunkle recommends the creation of a Family Counsel in the executive branch of government that would advocate for the interests of families and children by streamlining this flow of federal funding.

This is an interesting strategy of reforming the system because it attempts to fight fire with fire; the proposal would create a special interest group to counter the abuses of special interest groups that allegedly drive the funding of social service agencies (including education). In this perspective, the funding of education and social service agencies is defined by the politics of power and turf. Absent is any consideration of the problems of defining ownership, the costs of monitoring, and the impact of these issues on organizational structure.

Politicians, who are accountable to the taxpayers on election day if not every day, want a system of funding for social services that is manageable, not terribly costly, and effective. Collaborative ventures complicate the process of monitoring social service monies, because monies get pooled into other revenue streams for projects over which no single agency is accountable. Categorical funding strategies, derided by Dunkle and others as fostering counterproductive fragmentation, do provide legislators with the means by which to achieve accountability; these monies are legally restricted so that they can be used only for the targeted audience or program designated in the funding appropriation bill. As long as the cost of accountability is high and the outcomes of organizational activity difficult to assess, as with collaborative endeavors, legislators are likely to maintain support for a system of categorical funding.

Dunkle (1995) argues that the fragmented, categorical funding emanating from the federal government reinforces fragmentation at the state and local levels. As long as this funding arrangement is maintained and the system of accountability for program administrators at the state level are unchanged, it seems unlikely to expect individuals to significantly alter their behavior let alone an entire system of organizations. Precluding a system of reform that begins funding collaboratives without all the confusion of overlapping systems of accountability, the current system of fragmented, hierarchically structured organizations is likely to remain in place no matter how intensely administrators are cajoled to change.

This last point raises a fundamental issue, discussed by Barrot and Raybould in chapter 3, which is that systematic change will not be accomplished by incremental changes at the individual level. The problem is that the incentive structures and constraints facing an organization are different from those confronting individuals. In this case, expecting individual changes ignores the larger fiscal environment and the impact it has on how organizations are structured. If change is to be accomplished, the fiscal structure by which social and educational organizations are financed will have to be changed. This will be difficult due to the ownership issues discussed above; legislators will want assurances that the programs targeted by their resources will receive them, and collaboration diminishes the degree to which these assurances can be given.

CONCLUSIONS: PROMISES AND PITFALLS

The promise of interagency collaboration is that it offers educational and social service agencies access to an expanded pool of resources and expertise that otherwise would be difficult to acquire, especially given the fiscal conservatism of today's political environment. Access to these new and additional resources potentially enables these agencies to provide clients with a more comprehensive and appropriate set of services. These goals seem laudable and desirable. Moreover, collaboration seems like a fundamentally reasonable arrangement by which to pursue these goals.

The argument in this chapter is not with the assumed value of policies that promote and support collaboration. Rather, it is argued that the current arrangement by which social and educational agencies are funded requires a system of monitoring and accountability that locks these organizations into a hierarchical structure and precludes the horizontal relationships necessary for effective collaboration. The logic of the point suggests that unless there is significant change in the way educational and social service agencies are funded, monitored, and measured, there is little likelihood that the current efforts to promote collaboration as a reform for fragmented service sectors will succeed.

We need to recognize the organizational character of collaboratives and their economic facets (particularly the drive for efficiency and reduction of the organizational costs discussed in the paper). We need to recognize the vulnerability of administrators and their tendency to respond to the particular situations they face. We cannot change their attitudes and values; consequently we need to change the funding and structural arrangements by which administrators operate. If the incentive structure for the organization is appropriately restructured, then there is a greater chance that administrators will promote the long-term systemic changes so desperately needed if social and education services are actually going to serve the complex and inter-related needs of America's children and families.

One potential pitfall is that the current reform movement will continue to ask administrators and frontline workers to make changes in a system that operates with ingrained incentives and structures running counter to the direction of those changes. If such a strategy is pursued it is very likely that the future of collaboration will resemble its present state, which despite valiant individual efforts is unquestionably shy of achieving systemic change. Recognizing the problem of ownership and monitoring costs and the effect these factors have on how organizations structure themselves helps explain why the evaluation evidence of interagency collaboratives reveals limited and abandoned ventures. Limited ventures, superficial in character, hold relatively little risk of compromising the primary responsibilities of individual organizations for which they are held accountable by funding agencies. Such arrangements, however, are not likely to change the needs of families or the limitations of the current system to meet the expanded needs of those services.

In consideration of these factors the recommendation proposed in this paper supports government funding of these collaborative programs, which recognizes the costs of their operation and legitimizes their role in the institutional environment of existing service agencies. Such a funding arrangement would necessarily have to be designed to accommodate the operation and function of horizontally configured service organizations (differing radically from current hierarchical organizations). The proposal here would be to create a system of services specifically intended to foster and support interagency collaboration—a system not unlike the efforts undertaken during the 1960s to expand the role of regional educational service agencies. A key difference between the regional service agencies and the interagency service organizations proposed here is that the underlying philosophy of these new organizations would not be to create large scale program efforts but rather to tailor efficient programs (with an eye to costs and quality) that meet the needs of constituencies that existing service agencies are attempting to help. Accountability for these new agencies would have to be structured so that teams of people (the heart of reformed collaborative endeavors) were evaluated for long term goals and progress. In this way, budgeting and evaluation processes would serve as a means to help manage the ownership problem that has long been an issue for federally funded and state-funded organizations.

A second pitfall is associated with Callahan's observation that administrators vulnerable to societal criticisms are likely to respond in ways that look appropriate but may not lead to sustained and productive reform. This is particularly true with regard to collaboration because pursuing such ventures, when it is difficult to assess either the quality or effect of the intervention, leaves the administrator, in response to criticisms about inefficiency, struggling to reduce unit costs. Without careful consideration of the purposes of collaboration, there is the possibility that current practice will lead back to the cult of efficiency that Callahan so rightfully castigated.

Finally, a third potential pitfall is associated with Drucker's assertion that reforms are often initiated because of perceptions about inefficiency and waste. Over time, however, the reform takes on a moral quality that ignores the economic characteristics of decision making and organization. Thus, where reform was once seen as an alternative to current practice, it emerges as the status quo. Further, because it currently represents thinking about "best practice," which is believed to solve critical social problems, individual managers and frontline workers are encouraged to redouble their efforts when evidence that the current level of effort is having little effect. The end result is cyclic and disastrous.

The nature of collaborative organizations, and perhaps of all organizations, is that they are simultaneously social and economic in character. They are social in that they require people to come together, build trust, act together, and change the way they do their work. They are economic in that the rationale for collaboration is largely based on the premise that a collaborative organizational structure will enable social service providers to use their resources more effectively and thereby produce social services more efficiently. Collaboration is said to hold a comparative advantage over the conventional organization of individually operated service agencies. Failure to recognize and understand the dual nature of collaborative organizations runs the risk, according to Barney and Ouchi (1986, p. 3), "of either implementing programs that are not economically viable, or of choosing economically powerful programs that cannot be implemented."

REFERENCES

Alter, C., & Hage, J. (1993). *Organizations working together*. Newbury Park, CA: Sage.

Barney, J., & Ouchi, W. G. (1986). *Organizational economics: Toward a new paradigm for understanding and studying organizations*. San Francisco: Jossey-Bass.

Bendix, R. (1956). *Work and authority in industry*. New York: Wiley.

Bergquist, W., Betwee, J., & Meuel, D. (1995). *Building strategic relationships*. San Francisco: Jossey-Bass.

Brimelow, P. (1986). Are we spending too much on education? *Forbes, 138*, 72–76.

Bruner, C. (1991). *Thinking collaborative: Ten questions and answers to help policy makers improve children's services*. Washington, DC: Published by the Education and Human Services Consortium.

Callahan, R. E. (1962). *Education and the cult of efficiency: A study of the social forces that have shaped the administration of the public schools*. Chicago: University of Chicago Press.

Coase, R. H. (1937). The nature of the firm. *Economica, 4*, 386–405.

Crowson, R. L., & Boyd, W. L. (1992). Coordinated services for children: Problems of organization and implementation. *The CEIC Review, 1*(2), 3–5, 8.

Davis, P. (1976). *Educational Services Centers in the U S A*. Hartford: Connecticut State Department of Education.

Drucker, P. F. (1989). *The new realities*. New York: Harper & Row.

Dunkle, M. C. (1993). *Solving the maze of federal programs for children & families: Perspectives from key congressional staff*. Washington, DC: The Policy Exchange, The Institute for Educational Exchange.

Dunkle, M. C. (1994). *Linking schools with health & social services: Perspectives from Thomas Payzant on San Diego's New Beginnings*. Washington, DC: The Policy Exchange, The Institute for Educational Exchange.

Dunkle, M. C. (1995). *Who controls major federal programs for children and families: Rube Goldberg revisited*. Washington, DC: The Policy Exchange, The Institute for Educational Exchange.

Eisenberg, E. (1995). Communications in family-school partnerships. In L. C. Rigsby, M. C. Reynolds, & M. C. Wang (Eds.), *School community connections: Exploring issues for research and practice* (pp. 101–120). San Francisco: Jossey-Bass.

Evan, W. M. (1993). *Organization Theory: Research and Design*. New York: Macmillan.

Foundation, A. E. C. (1994). *Kids count data book: State profiles of child well being*. Washington DC: Annie E. Casey Foundation and the Center for the Study of Social Policy.

Gray, B. (1989). *Collaborating: Finding common ground for multiparty problems.* San Francisco: Jossey-Bass.

Gray, B. (1995). Obstacles to success in educational collaborations. In L. C. Rigsby, M. C. Reynolds, & M. C. Wang (Eds.), *School community connections: Exploring issues for research and practice* (pp. 71–99). San Francisco: Jossey-Bass.

Hall, R., Clark, J., Giordan, P., Johnson, P., & Roekel, M. (1977). Patterns of interorganizational relationships. *Administrative Science Quarterly, 22,* 445–474.

Hodgkinson, H. (1993). American education: The good, the bad, and the task. In S. Elam (Ed.), *The state of the nation's public schools: A conference report* (pp. 13–23). Bloomington, IN: Phi Delta Kappa.

Jones, B. L., & Maloy, R. W. (1988). *Partnerships for improving schools.* New York: Greenwood Press.

Kirst, M. W., & Kelley, C. (1995). Collaboration to improve education and children's services: Politics and policy making. In L. C. Rigsby, M. C. Reynolds, & M. C. Wang (Eds.), *School Community Connections: Exploring Issues for Research and Practice* (pp. 21–44). San Francisco: Jossey-Bass.

Kusserow, R. P. (1991). *Service integration: A twenty-year retrospective.* Washington, DC: U.S. Department of Health and Human Services, Office of Inspector General.

Levine, M., & Trachtman, R. (1988). *American business and the public school: case studies of corporate involvement in public education.* New York: Columbia University, Teachers College.

Lieberman, M. (1993). *Public education: An autopsy.* Cambridge, MA: Harvard University Press.

March, J. G., & Simon, H. A. (1958). *Organizations.* New York: Wiley.

Melaville, A. I., & Blank, M. J. (1993). *Together we can: A guide for crafting a profamily system of education and human services.* Washington, DC: U.S. Department of Education, Office of Educational Research and Improvement.

National Commission on Excellence in Education. (1983). *A nation at risk: The imperative for education reform.* Washington, DC: U.S. Department of Education.

Perrow, C. (1986). *Complex organizations: A critical essay* (3rd ed.). New York: McGraw-Hill.

Rigsby, L. C., Reynolds, M. C., & Wang, M. C. (Eds.). (1995). *School community connections: Exploring issues for research and practice.* San Francisco: Jossey-Bass.

Ringers, J. (1976). *Community/Schools and Interagency Programs: A Guide.* Midland, MI: Pendell.

Ripley, C. E. (1939). *Community schools in action.* New York: Viking Press.

Sarason, S. B., Carroll, C., Maton, K., Cohen, S., & Lorentz, E. (1977). *Human services & resource networks.* Cambridge, MA: Brookline Books.

Thomas, J. A. (1971). *The productive school: A systems analysis approach to educational administration.* New York: Wiley.

Williamson, O. E. (1986). *Economic organization: Firms, markets and policy control.* New York: New York University Press.

CHAPTER 5

Teacher Teams: Redesigning Teachers' Work for Collaboration

Diana G. Pounder

Many of today's school initiatives have been introduced to enhance the school organization or improve the quality of student and teacher outcomes. Among these reform and restructuring efforts, employee involvement strategies (e.g., site-based management, participative decision-making, shared decision influence) are among the most popular.

One approach to teacher involvement is to change the design of the work to enhance teacher motivation and involvement and other work outcomes (Mohrman & Lawler, 1992). Although individual job enhancement approaches were introduced during the 1980s to enrich teacher jobs (Hart, 1990), they have had limited impact because only a small number of teachers benefit and because the strong norm of egalitarianism in schools discourages individual teacher attention or distinction (Pounder, 1997).

A less utilized or studied approach to teacher work redesign is work group enhancement (Crow & Pounder, 1997; Pounder, 1995, 1997). Work groups or teacher teams are designed to increase members' responsibility for the group's performance and outcomes, creating work interdependence and opportunities for self-management. Work group members must develop interpersonal and group decision-making skills and often have greater control over a broader range of work issues. The clearest example of this may be found in some middle schools in which teachers are organized into interdisciplinary grade-level teams that have decision-making responsibilities for the educational program of a particular group of students. These decisions may include curricular emphasis and coordination, student management and behavioral interventions, student class assignment and flexible grouping strategies, student assessment, staffing decisions and assignments, curricular and co-curricular scheduling, coordinated parent communication, or budgetary allocations.

Additionally, because work group enhancement organizes work around students rather than departmental disciplines, there is a tighter connection between teachers' work and student outcomes. This allows teachers greater comprehensive knowledge of and responsibility for student learning and outcomes. This approach may be especially beneficial in secondary schools, where teachers' work and the educational experience of students is often fractionalized, with little coordination across subject areas and little knowledge and responsibility for comprehensive student learning (Boyer, 1983; Goodlad, 1984; Sizer, 1984). Also, work group enhancement has the benefit of involving all school educators in cooperative decision-making and organizational change. Some suggest that educational teams hold the potential to "rebuild schools"—as long as they maintain the focus on the educational needs of pupils rather than auxiliary issues (Maeroff, 1993, p. 519).

The purpose of this chapter is to discuss the potential for redesigning teachers' work to have a work group or team emphasis. The chapter presents a conceptual framework for effective work groups followed by an analysis and discussion of team work in schools, including related research on teacher teams. The chapter closes with "promises and pitfalls" of teacher work teams.

MODEL OF EFFECTIVE WORK GROUPS

Hackman and Oldham's work on job redesign (1980) probably represents the most comprehensive conceptualization of effective work groups to date (chaps. 7–8, pp. 161–218). The model of effective work groups describes the group structural elements, organizational context, and interpersonal processes which influence group effectiveness. Before exploring the specific elements of the model, it is important to understand how work groups and work group effectiveness are defined.

Literature on work teams or work groups uses a variety of different terms—such as self-managing work groups, self-determining work groups, or task-oriented work groups. These work groups are generally characterized by definitions and criteria similar to those established by Hackman and Oldham (1980, p. 165). That is:

> [Work groups are] intact (if small) social systems whose members have the authority to handle internal processes as they see fit in order to generate a specific group product, service, or decision. Such groups have the following three attributes.

1. They are *real* groups . . . members have interdependent relations with one another . . . they develop differentiated roles over time . . . the group is perceived as such both by members and nonmembers.

2. They are *work* groups. The group must have a defined piece of work to do that results in a product, service, or decision whose acceptability is at least potentially measurable . . .

3. They are *self-managing* groups. Group members must have the authority to manage their own task and interpersonal processes as they carry out their work.

Hackman and Oldham suggest that *effective* work groups are those: (1) whose output "meets or exceeds organizational standards of quantity and quality," (2) whose "members needs are more satisfied than frustrated," and (3) whose "social process maintains or enhances the capability of members to work together on subsequent tasks"—that is, the group doesn't "burn itself up" (168–170). They further specify that the group's effectiveness is largely determined by *intermediate effectiveness criteria*: the level of effort; amount of knowledge, skill, or expertise; and the appropriateness of performance strategies applied to the group work. The relative salience of each of these intermediate criteria in determining the group's effectiveness can vary—depending on the work technology. That is, all three intermediate criteria may not be equally important in determining the group's effectiveness for some types of work.

The model outlines the group structural elements (work design features), organizational context, and interpersonal processes that influence these intermediate criteria of effectiveness. Central to the model are the *group structural elements*. First among these is the *design of the group work or task*. Like individual jobs, group work should have high motivating potential. These work characteristics are derived from Hackman and Oldham's original job characteristics model (1980, p. 83), although the emphasis in this model is on the *group's work* rather than that of the individual. Work characteristics are:

1. Interaction and dealing with others (degree to which the job requires one to interact and deal with multiple others)

2. Work discretion or autonomy (freedom in scheduling or carrying out work assignments)

3. Skill variety (need for many different skills to accomplish job tasks)

4. Feedback from others (about one's work performance)

5. Feedback from the work itself (about one's work performance)

6. Task identity (completion of a "whole" and identifiable task and seeing the visible work outcome)

7) Task significance (degree to which a job affects others or their work in the organization; work interdependence)

In addition, group structural elements should include considerations of the *work group composition*. The authors indicate that the work group should:

1. include members who have a high degree of relevant work knowledge or expertise;

2. be large enough to do the work—but not much larger;

3. have members who have at least a moderate degree of interpersonal skills;

4. have a reasonable balance of homogeneity and heterogeneity in its membership (Hackman & Oldham, 1980, pp. 174–179)

Lastly, group structural elements should address the *group norms about performance processes*. That is, to the degree possible, conditions should be created that help the group "develop norms that reinforce the use of strategies that are uniquely appropriate to the group task, and that are amenable to change when task requirements or constraints change" (p. 181). Typically, group norms are not considered *structural* features of groups. However, this theory suggests that group norms about performance strategies serve as an informal control mechanism—helping shape individual members' behavior and reducing performance monitoring effort and time. Each of these group structural features is hypothesized to affect each of the respective intermediate effectiveness criteria. That is, the group work characteristics influence the group's work effort, the group composition influences the knowledge and expertise applied to the group work, and the group norms about performance processes influence the appropriateness of performance strategies applied to the group work.

The work group effectiveness model also addresses two other factors which influence group effectiveness: organizational context and interpersonal processes. *Supportive organizational contexts* include: (1) reward systems and control mechanisms (or performance monitoring systems) that are based on group performance rather than individual performance in achieving group objectives, (2) available relevant training and technical consultation, and (3) clear work requirements and constraints. *Healthy interpersonal processes* are those that increase "process gains" and reduce "process losses" (p. 200). That is, work coordination and communication processes that enhance group effectiveness include: (1) efficient coordination efforts and enhanced group commitment, (2) appropriate sharing and weighting of relevant knowledge and input from group members, and (3) implementing and inventing performance strategies. Again, each of these respective organizational context and interpersonal process variables are hypothesized to affect the respective intermediate effectiveness variables of work group effort, work group knowledge and expertise, and appropriate performance strategies.

Hackman and Oldham's conceptualization of effective work groups (1980) was articulated almost two decades ago, yet had received little empirical testing until the mid-1980s. Since that time, researchers have studied teamwork in business, industry, and other noneducational settings much more systematically than in educational organizations—perhaps because the use of work groups has occurred more in these other types of organizations. In 1990 Hackman collected twenty work team case studies to represent research findings from several types of noneducational organizations. Summarizing this work, he states that several themes cut across these case studies (pp. 480–488)—suggesting additional variables not presented in the original group work effectiveness theoretical framework. These themes include:

1. *Time and rhythm*: The way a group operates is often influenced by time deadlines or regular cycles of work activity. The more predictable these deadlines or work cycles are, the more effectively teams can plan and implement the necessary work activity.

2. *Self-fueling spirals*: Group effectiveness also seems to be influenced by the way the group gets started. That is, a certain self-fulfilling prophecy may take shape based on the way a group gets started. Groups that start strong are often perceived as such by group members as well as by others in the organization. Subsequent group attributions are favorable and the positive spiral of group performance continues. Conversely, a group that gets off to a bad start may not be able to overcome the downward spiral similarly set in motion.

3. *Authority*: The amount of decision-making authority a team may have can vary. Ambiguity about the areas and degree of decision authority as well as the balance of authority between the group and management can influence the effectiveness of the work group.

4. *Work content*: The content or nature of the group's work can influence the group's character. That is, human service work groups take on a different character than management teams, task forces, professional support groups, performing groups, customer service

teams, or production teams. Each team's work content offers certain unique risks and opportunities. For instance, human service teams may suffer from emotional drain and struggle for control of their own emotions and that of clients. "The primary risk is burnout; the alternative risk is that burnout will be avoided by objectifying the team's clients, which inevitably results in poorer quality service to them" (pp. 491–492). Conversely, the work of human service groups is inherently motivating due to the importance of helping people.

Hackman concludes with several recommendations:

1. Manage and supervise the work group as a team, not as a collection of individuals.

2. Keep a clear and appropriate balance between the authority of the team and that of management.

3. Establish specific and appropriate group structural features, because effective group structure tends to develop healthy group processes. Structural considerations include motivating work responsibilities, appropriate group composition, and clear and explicit specification of the team's authority and accountability.

4. Provide appropriate organizational support for the team—such as a group reward system, training, relevant work or organizational information, and necessary supplies, materials, and equipment.

5. Provide appropriate managerial coaching or intervention when a group is struggling. (pp. 493–504)

This brief outline of work group concepts and relationships does not adequately cover the full range of scholarship and issues relevant to work group effectiveness. However, as Hackman (1990) suggested, work content is an important factor in influencing the character of work groups. Therefore, it is important to focus on school work groups. How does the conceptual framework outlined above relate to group work in schools? What scholarship currently exists regarding work group effectiveness in education?

School Work Teams

There are several types of work groups or teams that may appear in schools. They include groups such as *management teams or school advisory groups*, whose chief responsibility is to advise the principal or other administrators in problem solving, planning, and decision making for school improvement (such as the teams described by Scarr, 1992). Management or advisory teams have become especially popular during the past decade as schools have increasingly emphasized site-based decision making. Membership may include representative teachers (e.g., department chairs or grade-level leaders), school support staff, and parents or community members (e.g., PTA leaders).

Another type of team is a *special services team*, whose primary responsibility is to oversee and make decisions about the evaluation, placement, and educational plans of exceptional students. Special services teams have been maintained largely since the mainstreaming or inclusion of special education students in traditional public schools in the 1970s. Members may include special education teachers, professional support staff (e.g., school psychologist, social worker, medical personnel, guidance counselor), administrators, representative parents, and others.

A third type of team is an *interdisciplinary instructional team*, whose chief responsibilities are: (1) to develop and implement interdisciplinary curriculum and teaching strategies, based on the developmental stage of the child; (2) to develop coordinated interventions and management strategies to address student learning and/or behavioral problems; and (3) to provide coordinated communication with parents. Interdisciplinary instructional teams appear almost exclusively in middle level schools and emerged in the late 1960s as a key component of the middle schools movement. By the late 1980s, approximately 40 percent of middle level schools were using interdisciplinary teaming (Clark & Clark, 1994, p. 26). The primary type of multidisciplinary team is composed of core academic teachers (e.g., language arts, social studies, math, science, reading) who are responsible for the required academic instruction of a contained group of a hundred or more students. Another instructional team(s) may include teachers from required exploratory or elective subject areas such as physical education, art, music, computers and technology, industrial arts, adult living skills (home economics), foreign languages, or other similar course offerings. Professional support staff such as guidance counselors, school psychologists, library and media specialists, special education teachers, reading specialists, or other learning specialists may be integrated into core and/or exploratory teams or may serve as consultants to all of the teams. School administrators typically serve in an advisory or consultant role to all teams, attending team meetings as needed or requested by team members.

Of the three types of teams presented above, interdisciplinary instructional teams may hold greatest promise for significant and substantive change in schools and their outcomes for students and teachers. Unlike other team or employee involvement strategies, interdisciplinary instructional teams: (1) involve all school faculty, changing the nature of teacher work itself; (2) directly affect the instruction of all school students; and (3) establish a close and direct link between the restructuring effort and student/school outcomes. These are particularly powerful characteristics, because the success of school restructuring efforts is limited unless schools organize in ways that are tied to the needs of learners and the teaching-learning process (Rowan, 1990). Below I will analyze and discuss the group structural elements (work design features), organizational context, and group processes of school interdisciplinary instructional teams and report available research results on teacher teams in schools.

GROUP STRUCTURAL ELEMENTS / WORK DESIGN FEATURES

Among the structural elements of school work groups, the *work characteristics* of teacher teams have received relatively more research attention. A recent study compared the work characteristics of middle level teachers who worked in teams to teachers with a traditional individual job design (Pounder, 1995). Teachers were asked to evaluate their work using Hackman and Oldham's job characteristics (1980), modified slightly for relevance to teachers' work in schools. Teachers working in teams reported that their work required significantly more skill variety and somewhat more interaction with others, task significance, feedback from the work itself, and work discretion/autonomy. Teaming teachers further indicated that they had more knowledge of students' academic performance and personal lives and had more contact with parents than did the nonteaming teachers. Teaming teachers also indicated they had significantly more knowledge of other teachers' work and experienced more help and work coordination from others than did their nonteaming counterparts.

These results were largely consistent with other scholarship on interdisciplinary team work, although no other studies have studied the same specific work characteristic variables. Erb (1995, pp. 181–182) reports that teaming reduces teacher isolation and focuses teachers' attention and coordinated action on student learning and behavior. Teachers especially target students with learning and/or behavioral problems, developing coordinated plans for intervention and changes in instructional practice, including parent conferences and other increased parental communication. Typically, teamed teachers have a common preparation period and a regular shared meeting time—at least weekly if not daily, explaining much of the increased interaction with others.

They have much more shared time to focus on problem solving, decision making, planning, and joint communication with parents. Erb reports that teacher teams tend to systematically address student problems earlier, communicating earlier and more frequently with parents than teachers who work in isolation (Erb, 1987). Further, when teacher teams observe similar performance problems among many students, they are more likely to become proactive in revising management or teaching strategies, developing and reenforcing consistent team expectations and routines, and rewarding appropriate behavior to reduce student management problems (Erb, 1995, p. 185). In fact, teacher teams become so effective in handling student behavioral problems that team schools report significantly fewer office referrals or suspensions than do non-team schools (Crow & Pounder, 1997; George & Oldaker 1985).

Additionally, teaming teachers spend more time talking with others about curricular and co-curricular issues and, after working together for a year or more, have greater knowledge of the curriculum and instructional matters beyond the limits of their own content area (Erb, 1988, 1995). Teachers who work together for longer periods often integrate their instruction to the point of abandoning traditional subject areas for curricula based on personal or social themes (Erb & Doda, 1989; Hawkins & Graham, 1994), although some researchers have indicated that curricular coordination is one of the last points of work integration achieved (Arhar, Johnston, & Markle, 1988; Beane, 1993; Lipsitz, 1984). Teachers' work-related interaction increases also with professional support staff members and school administrators (Erb, 1995, p. 184).

Most scholarship on interdisciplinary teacher teams suggests that teamed teachers have greater autonomy and discretion in how they do their work than do their nonteaming counterparts; they particularly have greater discretion in grouping students for instruction and greater flexibility in scheduling instructional time. Typically, interdisciplinary teacher teams are assigned a group of a hundred or more students and the core academic subjects are scheduled in a collective block of time (e.g., four or more hours) rather than distinct subject periods of forty-five to fifty minutes each. Thus, teacher teams typically have discretion regarding student grouping and instructional scheduling within the team block. Teachers may group or regroup students to meet learner needs for different lessons, offering greater individual customization of learning activities. Also, they have flexibility regarding scheduling instructional activities within the team block (Erb, 1995, p. 187; George & Oldaker, 1985). For instance, teachers may want to show an eighty-minute film to all students concurrently and then follow this with small group discussions. This type of flexibility is not available in traditional class periods. Thus, teacher teams may exercise greater discretion in scheduling their work activities.

Collectively, scholarship on teacher work groups largely suggests that team work is more enriched and has greater motivating potential than does traditional teacher work with an individual emphasis. For participating teachers, well-designed team work can increase:

1. work-related communication and problem solving with others
2. discretion in scheduling students and instructional time
3. knowledge of other curricular areas and instructional strategies
4. feedback from the work itself and from others
5. knowledge of students and contribution to their total educational experience
6. interdependence and work coordination with others

A second important structural element of work groups is the *group's composition*. Interdisciplinary teams have, by design, a high degree of diverse professional knowledge and expertise. Because teachers from multiple content areas compose the team, they bring not only varied subject expertise but also varied instructional methods and strategies. A team which includes professional support staff or learning specialists may have even greater knowledge and expertise among its members. Also, teachers and other educator team members are likely to bring a high degree of interpersonal skills to the group work. As with any work group, it is important for teachers to receive training about group processes including effective listening and communication skills. However, compared to many work groups that have been studied in non-educational settings, groups composed of school personnel have self-selected a profession that requires a high degree of interaction with others, service to others, and professional training, often including human interaction skills. Thus, it is reasonable to expect that due to occupational self-selection and training, most teachers have at least a moderate (if not high) degree of interpersonal skills.

A balance or appropriate mix of member homogeneity versus heterogeneity is sometimes difficult to establish on interdisciplinary teams. Unless a school is new, faculty members are typically not recruited and selected expressly to work or serve on a particular team. Rather, most teams "inherit" their members from existing school personnel—who may or may not be assigned to a team based on a balance of teaching experience, team experience, gender, race, or other important member characteristics. Historical, political, or seniority priorities may influence team assignments more than considerations of team balance unless there is specific precedent or policy allowing teacher transfer and assignment to promote team or school effectiveness. However, as a school experiences turnover due to voluntary transfers, retirements, or resignations, schools can recruit and select team members who will provide the appropriate balance and skills necessary for team work.

Observation of work teams in a middle school suggests that experience may be among the more important "balance" variables to consider in assigning members to teams (Crow & Pounder, 1997). Specifically, it is important to consider different types of experience, such as quantity and variety of teaching experience, experience working in the school and/or grade level, and experience working in teams. Experienced and senior teachers in the school can enhance team expertise about "how the system works." Experienced team teachers may help colleagues see "the vision" of teaming possibilities that those new to teaming may not be able to imagine. However, "the best composition seems to be that of individuals who are somewhat different in attitudes, backgrounds, and experiences, *but not radically different*" (Seamon, 1981, p. 45, citing Lifton, 1972, p. 192).

Research on interdisciplinary teams does not suggest an ideal group size as long as the group is "within the range of two to eight" members (Erb, 1995, p. 193). Several problems may arise if the group size is too large or too small (Seamon, 1981, pp. 42–43). For instance, if groups are too large, communication patterns and organizational arrangements become too complex, thus increasing the inefficiencies and "process losses" that Hackman and Oldham (1980) describe. Also, if the group is too large, work responsibilities can become distributed so thinly that members may feel less responsibility for the group work and may engage in more "shirking" behavior. By contrast, if the group is too small for the assigned task or responsibilities, members may feel overwhelmed and unable to complete the work. Because most school interdisciplinary teams include one teacher from each of four or five subject areas (Clark & Clark, 1994, p.128) plus perhaps two or three professional support personnel, these teams are not likely to develop the problems of excessively large or small groups.

Scholarship indicates that teamed teachers are involved in more types of decisions that affect the operation of the school (Erb, 1987; George & Oldaker 1985; Lipsitz, 1984), although how teams specifically establish *group norms about performance processes* is difficult to assess. Presumably, interdisciplinary teams have considerably more discretion to establish how they do their work and to develop strategies that are more effective or efficient in addressing their work responsibilities. However, because many teachers have been unaccustomed to exercising decision-making discretion in scheduling students and instructional time, coordinating interdisciplinary instruction, and working cooperatively with others to establish consistent student expectations and routines beyond their own classroom, new teacher teams may fail to break old work norms to establish new ways to do their work. Pounder recently observed teacher teams in their second year of implementation and noted that teachers failed to exercise as much work discretion and decision-making authority as they could (Crow & Pounder, 1997). This author is reminded of her own experience as a school principal who implemented teacher teaming in a middle school. During the first few weeks of initial team meetings, teachers did not seem to understand that they had the freedom to set their own agenda for team meetings and to use the time in ways that helped them carry out their work more effectively or efficiently. In fact, if the principal was detained in the office, teachers would disband the team meeting within five minutes. However, by the second semester of the school year, teachers would conduct all their team business even when the principal did not attend the meeting at all. It took them several months to fully exercise the discretion and authority that they had as a team.

It is even more difficult to assess the degree to which these performance process norms serve as a control mechanism to monitor and shape performance behaviors. Certainly teachers develop more knowledge of one another's work performance and contributions to the team and thus have the potential for monitoring or shaping performance behavior. In recent interviews with newly teamed teachers, one teacher noted that teaming required members to share information about their classroom teaching—and that some teachers seemed reluctant or afraid to share this information, perhaps because they felt vulnerable about the judgments of other team members (Crow & Pounder, 1997). This observation suggests that the team and its work norms can potentially influence others' performance behaviors, although it is unclear specifically how this happens or is effectively facilitated.

ORGANIZATIONAL CONTEXT

A supportive organizational context is important to any restructuring effort. One important organizational factor is *performance monitoring and rewards*. Literature on interdisciplinary teacher teams makes little mention of monitoring or reward systems modified to match the nature of group work. Few schools have adopted Hackman's recommendation that teams should be treated as a *group* rather than a collection of individuals (1990). That is, performance monitoring and rewards within a school are seldom based on the attainment of team objectives. This may be because performance supervision and evaluation policies are typically established at the school district level, with uniform practices across the district. In fact, schools may exercise little discretion about how personnel are evaluated—as individuals or as a group. Also, schools have notoriously limited reward systems. Most school districts do not have traditional merit pay systems and unless there is a true career ladder program, teachers have few opportunities for promotion within the teaching role. Often the only reward that can be offered teachers—as individuals or as groups—is favorable public or organizational recognition and formal or informal expressions of appreciation.

This area of school personnel practices is ripe for change, especially in view of school restructuring to enhance group work. To improve group performance monitoring and rewards, work groups themselves may best initiate proposals for alternative supervision and reward systems. Peer and self-evaluation of *group* performance in addition to administrative review of group performance offer one alternative approach. Individual performance assessment may be important only for inexperienced nontenured teachers, although peer reviews by team colleagues may be an important source of additional performance data beyond traditional data sources. The current norms and practices regarding teacher supervision and evaluation may not be easy to change without considerable controversy. However, an emphasis on group performance rather than individual performance may offer opportunities for schools to address some of the shortcomings of current teacher appraisal systems (Duke, 1995).

Available task-relevant training and technical consultation for work groups is a critical organizational support in schools as well as in noneducational organizations. Most schools spend a full year or more preparing and training teachers for the transition to interdisciplinary teacher teams. Team literature particularly emphasizes the importance of professional development to improve such relevant work skills as interpersonal communication skills, group decision-making skills, effective meeting strategies, goal-setting and evaluation, interdisciplinary instructional planning, and adolescent development (Clark & Clark, 1994, pp. 240–266; Erb, 1995, p. 192; Haimes, 1995, p. 77; Wilkinson & Smith, 1995, p. 108). Schools often send their faculty to observe and talk with teachers in teaming schools and may bring in consultants to lead faculty in team-building activities to help teachers build commitment and identification with their teams.

As suggested by Hackman (1990), the way a group gets started (self-fueling spirals) may have a strong influence on its long-term success. Further, because teams may go through several developmental stages (Garner, 1995, pp. 11–12; George, 1982; Pickler, 1987), their training and professional development needs may vary over time. Fully-functioning teams may take three years or more to develop (Erb & Doda, 1989). In fact, teaming changes need to be planned in stages with implementation staggered over time to keep from overwhelming the faculty (Crow & Pounder, 1997; Erb, 1995, p. 190). Secondary teachers who see themselves as content specialists may be particularly resistant to curricular integration or other team coordination efforts (Clark & Clark, 1994). Change literature suggests that educational innovations typically progress from focus on self (the teacher) to focus on the task to a focus on the impact to students (Hall, Loucks, Rutherford, & Newlove, 1975; Hord, Rutherford, Huling-Austin, & Hall, 1987). As a result, teaming may best begin with a focus on team management issues (e.g., consistent team expectations for student behavior, policies and practices for flexible student grouping, a variety of schedule alternatives within block time, compatible procedures for evaluating student work, coordinated communication procedures with parents, etc.) then progress to a focus on cooperative teaching and curricular integration (Erb, 1995). (See also Evans-Stout, chap. 7, this text.)

Ongoing technical consultation needs may also change over time, but among the most important is knowledge about the cognitive and social-emotional development of students (at a particular age range) and the implications for teaching and learning (Clark & Clark, 1994). In fact, the hallmark of the middle school movement is the focus on teacher teamwork to address early adolescent developmental and learning needs. Although teachers typically have substantial knowledge about their content areas, they often find themselves with limited knowledge about child development and learning theories. This author has frequently seen teams wrestle with problems of student academic performance due to lack of knowledge about how some students may learn. However, I have never seen a team have trouble with teaching and learning issues due to lack of subject area knowledge. Also, as teacher teams assume greater decision authority, they may need ongoing consultation about school and district policies, legal considerations regarding student management and instruction, or other typical administrative information. It is incumbent on the school administrator and other professional support staff to provide a steady flow of task-relevant information to teachers to help improve the quality of their decision making and planning. (See also Crow, chapter 8, this text).

A third organizational support is *clear work requirements and constraints*. Specifically, teachers need a clear delineation of a team's *decision authority zone* relative to that of school or district administrative personnel. Also, formal team leadership needs to be established early on, because teams with designated leaders function better than leaderless groups (MacIver, 1990). Teams typically assume decision authority in arenas such as team goal-setting and managerial procedures, student placement and grouping, instructional time allocation, team interventions to address student learning and behavior problems, reward systems for team students, and other instructional and managerial decision areas. However, because teamed teachers may exercise greater influence in school-wide decisions (Erb, 1987), teachers need to understand the parameters of their decision authority and may, in fact, need to be encouraged to expand their zones of decision authority to maximize the potential of the work team. Ironically, teamed teachers in Pounder's study (1995) reported some decision deprivation, although observation data suggested that they had missed many opportunities to exercise the decision authority they had been given (Crow & Pounder, 1997).

In parallel fashion, teachers must understand the team's corresponding *group accountability* for their shared decisions. Teams can have little credibility with administrators, parents, or others if they fail to be accountable for their group decisions or actions. Teachers and administrators who are embarking on teaming arrangements need to consider and discuss fully their expectations regarding the balance of decision authority and accountability in the school. The quality of instructional management and teaching decisions are likely to be better when teachers are fully engaged in team decision-making and fully exercising their decision authority and corresponding group accountability (Erb, 1995, p. 187).

Another critical organizational support for interdisciplinary instructional teams is appropriate *allocation of time for instruction and meeting/planning*. In the most effective interdisciplinary team arrangements, a discrete group of students is assigned to a common academic block of instructional time with a core team of teachers. Failure to provide block scheduling dramatically undermines instructional options and the overall effectiveness and efficiency of teaming efforts. Teams may choose to work directly with administrators and guidance counselors responsible for master scheduling and student class assignments to assure an appropriate schedule for effective teaming. Similarly, teachers must be given a common time for team meetings and instructional planning. It is often considered impossible to arrange a time during the school day for teachers to work together; however, building master schedules to establish a common preparation period is usually not too difficult. Strategies to find additional time for team meetings is sometimes more difficult. Options may include double "preparation periods" to allow for daily meeting time, early release of students one day per week, or release of teachers from traditional lunchroom or playground supervision assignments to accommodate meeting time.

Many of these latter arrangements may require considerable support from school boards due to the additional financial costs or instructional time losses associated with these alternatives.

GROUP PROCESSES

An interdependent relationship often exists between group processes, group structure, and organizational context. Thus, some of Hackman and Oldham's *healthy interpersonal processes* have been addressed in the preceding analysis and discussion of group structural features and organizational support mechanisms. For example, *coordinating efforts* may be enhanced (with more "process gains" and fewer "process losses") when block scheduling and regular team meetings and preparation time are provided. When individuals must coordinate their work with others, communication mechanisms and organizational structures should be designed to reduce coordination "costs." Besides some of the structural or organizational features mentioned above, today's teacher teams are able to use computer technology to simplify communication and coordination. For example, e-mail can simplify routine communication with multiple individuals or groups: team members themselves, other teams, professional support personnel, and administrators (and students if they have regular access to school computers). Team meeting minutes, work deadlines, agendas, newsletter information, or other types of routine communication can be disseminated electronically for easy access by others. Also, a school computer network can enable teams to maintain a common electronic bulletin board or calendars or disseminate notices of upcoming events, joint instructional plans, or any documents that make communication about team endeavors easier. Even when teachers have this technological advantage, they may be unaccustomed to using it and may fail to see appropriate opportunities to reduce their communication and coordinating "process losses." Pounder's recent observations of one school's team meetings verified that teachers may be slow to realize the multiple uses and advantages of their new computer network. However, over time they began to use the computers more and more to facilitate communication and coordination efforts (Crow & Pounder, 1997).

Team commitment may be fostered through initial and ongoing faculty development activities as described above. Because teams should represent a microcosm of the school and reduce the size of the school for students, some teams spend considerable time building team identity for its teachers and students (Erb, 1995, p. 194). In fact, research suggests that students at teamed schools have higher levels of social bonding with peers, teachers, and their schools (Arhar, 1990); feel less anonymity and isolation (Clark, & Clark, 1994, p. 125); and have higher levels of self-concept (Stefanich, Wills, & Buss, 1991) than do their nonteaming counterparts. Similarly, teaming teachers experience greater work satisfaction (Arhar et al., 1988), sense of professionalism (Lipsitz, 1984), and professional efficacy (Ashton & Webb, 1986; Doda, 1984) than do nonteaming teachers. Interdisciplinary instructional teams may use methods not unlike athletic teams to build commitment and team identity. Teams often have contests to select their team name, colors, motto, or other group symbols. These symbols are further reinforced by displaying them on newsletters, T-shirts, team prizes, or other group rewards given to students or teachers.

Work group effectiveness is substantially reduced if all members are not actively involved in *sharing knowledge, work responsibilities, and other group inputs.* Crow and Pounder (1997) observed that teams vary substantially in their balance and distribution of input and task assignments among team members. One team, composed largely of the more experienced senior teachers in the school, typically had most (if not all) members actively engaged in problem-solving and decision-making discussions. Further, when action plans were completed, all teachers readily volunteered for different tasks with seldom any prodding by the team leader. Teachers seemed to easily recognize their area of expertise or interest relative to that of others, and each volunteered his/her service for their respective areas of task skill or interest. Thus, the work of the group was very evenly distributed across members. There were no shirkers or inactive members in the group. By contrast, one group's discussions were conducted largely by about half of the group members, the other half consistently sitting in silence, with little or no input even when prodded. Further, when necessary tasks were identified to complete a team activity, only two or three teachers consistently volunteered to do the work. One or two others would occasionally volunteer if prodded, and the remaining members seldom volunteered (or were assigned) any group task. Interviewees indicated that this pattern had also been present the first year of team implementation, but the previous year's most active team members had begun to withhold their ideas, knowledge, and service because they had come to resent the work imbalance in the group. During the second year of implementation, a different two or three teachers were carrying the burden of most of the team work. As a result, the team was "burning up" its most active and involved members due to the very uneven distribution of team work across its members.

The balance of group input may be addressed in a number of ways, including staff development to enhance group decision-making and communication skills. Also, when a group experiences an imbalance in member contributions, the team may need to confront the problem directly and decide what mechanisms they would like to use to establish a better balance of member inputs. There can be many reasons for the imbalance, thus the appropriate remedy may vary. However, confronting the problem openly and honestly is more likely to reveal an appropriate solution than letting the pattern go on indefinitely, resulting in a self-fueling downward spiral.

*Group effectiveness can be enhanced when teams *implement and invent performance strategies* that appropriately meet the team's work objectives. Teachers in traditional work assignments do not have much instructional influence beyond their classroom. However, teaming teachers learn to also develop co-curricular activities that reinforce interdisciplinary classroom instruction. For example, teachers in the middle school in which this author served conducted a mock presidential election during a regular presidential election year. Students auditioned to role-play each of the Democratic and Republican presidential and vice-presidential candidates by writing and giving a speech to their English class group. After the candidate actors and their respective running mates were selected, team students attended a "political rally" and "debate" in which candidates gave their campaign speeches to the team and students asked relevant political questions derived from their social studies course work. Selected students also assumed the roles of recognized television journalists to conduct postdebate candidate interviews and commentary that were aired on the within-school television network. Co-curricular activities such as these can make instruction real and relevant to students, offering teaching and learning opportunities seldom considered in nonteamed schools.

Similarly, team teachers can develop co-curricular clubs that engage in activities to reinforce classroom instruction; for example, a journalism club that writes a regular student newsletter, an arts club that paints colorful murals in the hallways, a crafts club in which students teach one another techniques for completing different craft or visual arts projects, or a music club that forms a small jazz band or mixed vocal quartet. Because newly developed teams may not have models for how teamwork or interdisciplinary instruction may be handled, they may best benefit from consultation with teachers who have successfully worked in teams for several years. Observation and direct interaction can give team members a wealth of detailed information about work strategies and new ways to approach instruction. (E-mail links can also allow ongoing communication and consultation as needed by the new team.)

In addition to the group process issues addressed above, many education and human relations books address problems with group interpersonal processes such as conflict, apathy, or other potentially ineffective group dynamics (e.g., Bertcher, 1994; Friend & Cook, 1992;

Harvey & Drolet, 1994; Seamon, 1981; and Worchel, Wood, & Simpson, 1992). Readers are encouraged to consult these books about many group process issues that are too lengthy to cover in this chapter.

PROMISES AND PITFALLS OF
TEACHER TEAMS: A SUMMARY

The analysis and discussion of work group effectiveness factors and research results on school interdisciplinary teams is encouraging in many regards. However, it is important to remember that these types of teams have been introduced almost exclusively in middle level schools as a part of the middle school movement. The adaptability of a team work design to other school levels is untested.

Group work may hold greater potential for meaningful change in secondary schools than in elementary schools for the following reasons. First, most elementary teachers already have the advantage of knowing and teaching "the whole child" across multiple curricular areas and developmental activities. They also have contact with students for significant blocks of time and can exercise greater flexibility in scheduling instructional time than secondary teachers who are locked into class periods of forty-five or fifty minutes. Communication between home and school is simpler because it typically involves only one teacher communicating with a child's parents. Also, because elementary students are largely taught in self-contained classrooms, the focus is more typically on the child than on separate and often disjointed curricular areas. By contrast, traditional secondary schools with their focus on curricular specialization may create disjointed educational experiences for students who feel disengaged from their multiple teachers and the school environment. Parents may experience secondary schools as complex environments where home-school communication is complicated and random at best, providing little coordinated information about their child or his/her educational experiences. Thus, interdisciplinary teams may hold greater promise for meaningful and substantial change in secondary schools than in elementary schools.

Are teacher teams likely to be effective work groups? What are the promises and pitfalls of interdisciplinary teacher teams? The following summary highlights the potential and the limitations of redesigning teachers' work to have a team emphasis, and it is written largely with secondary schools in mind.

Group Structural Elements or Work Design Features

Redesigning teachers' work to have a team emphasis promises to enrich teacher work characteristics and improve the motivating potential of the work. More specifically, well-designed team work can increase the following for teachers: (1) work-related interaction and problem solving with others (*dealing with others*); (2) discretion in how they do their work, including scheduling students and instructional time (*work discretion or autonomy*); (3) knowledge of other curricular areas and instructional strategies (*skill variety*); (4) feedback from the work itself and from others (*feedback*); (5) knowledge of students and contribution to their total educational experience (*task identity*); and (6) interdependence and work coordination with others (*task significance*).

Teacher teams promise to offer a high degree of diverse professional knowledge and at least a moderate to high degree of interpersonal skills, thus enhancing the amount of knowledge and skill applied to instruction. However, because schools may have limited discretion in how teachers are initially assigned to teams, the team composition may not be optimal in terms of moderate heterogeneity on some important variables (e.g., experiences, attitudes, backgrounds). Most interdisciplinary teams can be designed to have an appropriate and effective group size.

Teacher teams have the potential to develop group norms that would improve the appropriateness of work performance strategies. However, because teachers may be unaccustomed to thinking about new ways to do their work, teacher teams may need encouragement to fully explore and develop new approaches to student instruction. Also, teachers may be reluctant to try to influence (directly or indirectly) the performance behaviors of other teachers due to the strongly held norms of academic freedom, faculty autonomy, and egalitarianism that often exist in schools. In other words, existing norms about how the work of schools is conducted may inhibit the development of new, more effective performance norms.

Organizational Context

The performance evaluation and reward systems that exist in schools are not designed for a work group emphasis (other than whole school recognition). Further, schools have notoriously limited reward systems of any type. Thus, without substantial revision, current school performance monitoring systems and rewards are not likely to enhance the level of effort teachers would bring to team responsibilities.

Most schools that implement teacher teams are reasonably thorough in their initial training and development activities. However, schools may falter when it comes to ongoing training and consultation to help teams through the natural developmental stages to becoming a fully functioning team. Further, teams may particularly need more training regarding learning theory and the developmental stage of the children with whom they work. Some school districts may not have the resources to provide much support beyond the initial implementation phase of teaming, thus limiting the knowledge and skill teachers may apply to their group responsibilities.

Teachers may need encouragement to fully exercise the decision authority they have as a team. However, they must also understand the parameters of the team's authority. This understanding must be reached through direct and ongoing interaction and negotiation with the building principal or other school administrative authorities. The principal and the school district must come to terms with the changing balance of authority necessitated when teachers' jobs are redesigned to have a team emphasis (see also Crow, chapter eight, this text). Also, teacher teams must learn to assume accountability for their group decisions. This may lead to an uncomfortable awakening for teachers who, as individual teachers with limited authority over school decisions, have grown to expect the unconditional support and protection of their building principal. As the team exercises greater decision authority in the school or subschool, its members must likewise accept greater public accountability.

One of the most important supports an organization must provide if interdisciplinary teams are to be effective is adequate time for the team to meet during the work day. Most schools should have no trouble providing a shared preparation time for core teachers on the team. However, some schools may have difficulty providing the resources to give teachers additional time daily or even weekly for team meetings, joint parent conferences, or other shared activities.

Group Processes

Effective coordination and communication is the heart and soul of group work. Teacher teams must develop communication tools and coordination approaches that limit "process losses." If it becomes more difficult or time consuming, or requires more effort for teachers to work collectively than as individuals, then teamwork will "cost" too much to maintain (see also Galvin, chap. 4, this text). Several tools that can effectively reduce process losses in coordination and communication are block schedules, shared preparation periods, daily or weekly team meetings during the school day, and e-mail or other communication technologies that reduce the "costs" of working effectively as a team. Also, team commitment can be enhanced through ongoing training and development activities and attention to group identification activities, rewards, and so forth. In sum, teachers must experience more advantages than disadvantages to participating in the team if their work effort is to be enhanced.

The balance of work inputs by team members is critical to its success and is closely related to the team's composition. Although some teams may find it easy to maintain a similar level of team participation among its members, other teams may need help confronting problems of imbalance. Teams experiencing an imbalance in member participation should confront the problem directly, perhaps with the facilitation of the principal or some other outside consultant.

Although teacher teams may initially find it challenging to think of new or more appropriate ways to approach their instructional responsibilities, teams may eventually experience the freedom and innovative potential that teaming brings to both their curricular and co-curricular planning and instruction. Many teachers learn that their instructional strategies are much less limited as interdisciplinary team members than as individual teachers. This potential is stimulating and motivates teachers to address educational problems more creatively than before possible.

Redesigning teachers' work to have a work group or team emphasis offers an encouraging alternative to other employee involvement strategies in schools. Restructuring teachers' work and schools to promote interdisciplinary teaming is a reform that is closely tied to the core technology of schools—teaching and learning—and promises favorable outcomes for students as well as for teachers and others. However, this work redesign must be implemented carefully to avoid some of the pitfalls that may accompany collaborative work design.

REFERENCES

Arhar, J. M. (1990). Interdisciplinary teaming as a school intervention to increase the social bonding of middle level students. In J. L. Irvin (Ed.), *Research in middle level education: Selected studies 1990*. Columbus, OH: National Middle School Association.

Arhar, J. M., Johnston, J. H., & Markle, G. C. (1988). The effects of teaming and other collaborative arrangements. *Middle School Journal, 19*(4), 22–25.

Ashton, P. T., & Webb, R. B. (1986). *Making a difference: Teachers' sense of efficacy and student achievement*. New York: Longman.

Beane, J. A. (1993). *A middle school curriculum: From rhetoric to reality* (2nd ed.). Columbus, OH: National Middle School Association.

Bertcher, H. J. (1994). *Group participation: Techniques for leaders and members* (2nd ed.). Thousand Oaks, CA: Sage.

Boyer, E. L. (1983). *High school: A report on secondary education in America*. New York: Harper & Row.

Clark, S. N., & Clark, D. C. (1994). *Restructuring the middle level school: Implications for school leaders*. Albany, NY: SUNY Press.

Crow, G., & Pounder, D. G. (1997). *Faculty teams: Work group enhancement as a teacher involvement strategy.* Paper presented at a meeting of the American Educational Research Association, Chicago, IL.

Duke, D. L. (Ed.). (1995). *Teacher evaluation policy: From accountability to professional development.* Albany, NY: SUNY Press.

Doda, N. M. (1984). *Teacher perspectives and practices in two organizationally different middle schools.* Unpublished doctoral dissertation, University of Florida, Gainesville.

Erb, T. O. (1987). What team organization can do for teachers. *Middle School Journal, 18*(4), 3–6.

Erb, T. O. (1988). Focusing back on the child by liberating the teacher. *TEAM: The Early Adolescence Magazine, 2*(3), 10–18.

Erb, T. O. (1995). Teamwork in middle school education. In H. G. Garner (Ed.), *Teamwork models and experience in education* (pp. 175–198). Boston: Allyn & Bacon.

Erb, T. O., & Doda, N. M. (1989). *Team organization: Promise—practices and possibilities.* Washington, DC: NEA.

Friend, M., & Cook, L. (1992). *Interactions: Collaboration skills for school professionals.* New York: Longman.

Garner, H. G. (1995). *Teamwork models and experience in education.* Boston: Allyn & Bacon.

George, P. S. (1982). Interdisciplinary team organization: Four operational phases. *Middle School Journal, 13*(3), 10–13.

George, P. S., & Oldaker, L. L. (1985). *Evidence for the middle school.* Columbus, OH: National Middle School Association.

Goodlad, J. I. (1984). *A place called school.* New York: McGraw-Hill.

Hackman, J. R. (Ed.). (1990). *Groups that work (and those that don't): Creating conditions for effective teamwork.* San Francisco: Jossey-Bass.

Hackman, J. R., & Oldham, G. R. (1980). *Work redesign.* Reading, MA: Addison-Wesley.

Haimes, R. (1995). Planning for change. In H. G. Garner (Ed.), *Teamwork models and experience in education* (pp. 73–84). Boston: Allyn & Bacon.

Hall, G. E., Loucks, S. F., Rutherford, W. L., & Newlove, B. N. (1975). Levels of the use of the innovation: A framework for analyzing innovation adoption. *Journal of Teacher Education, 24*(1), 52–56.

Hart, A. W. (1990). Work redesign: A review of literature for education reform. In S. B. Bacharach (Ed.), *Advances in Research and Theories of School Management and Educational Policy* (Vol. 1, pp. 3–69). Greenwich, CT: JAI Press.

Harvey, T. R., & Drolet, B. (1994). *Building teams, building people.* Lancaster, PA: Technomic.

Hawkins, M., & Graham, D. (1994). *Curriculum architecture: Creating a place of our own.* Columbus, OH: National Middle School Association.

Hord, S. M., Rutherford, W. L., Huling-Austin, L., & Hall, G.E. (1987). *Taking charge of change.* Alexandria, VA: ASCD.

Lifton, W. M. (1972). *Groups: Facilitating individual growth and societal change.* NY: Wiley.

Lipsitz, J. S. (1984). *Successful schools for young adolescents*. New Brunswick, NJ: Transaction Books.

MacIver, D. (1990). Meeting the needs of young adolescents: Advisory groups, interdisciplinary teams, and school transition programs. *Phi Delta Kappan, 71*, 458–464.

Maeroff, G. (1993). Building teams to rebuild schools. *Phi Delta Kappan, 74*, 512–519.

Mohrman, S. A., & Lawler, E. E. (1992). Applying employee involvement in schools. *Educational Evaluation & Policy Analysis, 14*, 347–360.

Pickler, G. (1987). The evolutionary development of interdisciplinary teams. *Middle School Journal, 18*(2), 6–7.

Pounder, D. G. (1995, October). *Faculty work teams: Paradoxical influences on teachers' work, work experiences, and attitudes*. Paper presented at the annual meeting of the University Council for Educational Administration, Salt Lake City, UT.

Pounder, D. G. (1997). Teacher teams: Promoting teacher involvement and leadership in secondary schools. *The High School Journal, 80*(2), 117–124.

Rowan, B. (1990). Applying conceptions of teaching to organizational reform. In R. Elmore (Ed.), *Restructuring schools: The next generation of educational reform* (pp. 31–58). San Francisco: Jossey-Bass.

Scarr, L. E. (1992). Using self-regulating work teams. *Educational Leadership, 50*(3), 68–70.

Seamon, D. F. (1981). *Working effectively with task-oriented groups*. New York: McGraw-Hill.

Sizer, T. R. (1984). *Horace's compromise: The dilemma of the American high school*. Boston: Houghton Mifflin.

Stefanich, G. P., Wills, F. A., & Buss, R. R. (1991). The use of interdisciplinary teaming and its influence on student self-concept in the middle school. *Journal of Early Adolescence, 11*(4), 404–419.

Wilkinson, A. M., & Smith, M. (1995). Team recruitment, team building, and skill development. In H. G. Garner (Ed.), *Teamwork models and experience in education* (pp. 103–124). Boston: Allyn & Bacon.

Worchel, S., Wood, W., & Simpson, J. A. (Eds.). (1992). *Group process and productivity*. Newbury Park, CA: Sage.

CHAPTER 6

Marshaling Forces:
Collaboration across Educator Roles

Ann Weaver Hart

The school most American adults attended was organized simply by modern standards. The professionals in the school included a teacher or group of teachers and a principal. The local school board, often parents or their friends and acquaintances from the community, governed school affairs. As American schools and communities have become more diverse and the problems confronted by schools more complex, the professionals who have joined teachers and principals in their work have become similarly more diverse and more differentiated.

Increased interest in collaboration by these diverse professionals can be traced to demands for improved outcomes for students. Concentrating their focus on consultation and collaboration for special needs children, Thomas, Correa, and Morsink (1995) argued that schools can no longer afford to neglect collaboration as they seek to address "the complex needs of students in general or special education because the needs of individual students are too complex to be handled by a single professional working in isolation" (p. iv). They remind their readers that increased cultural diversity complicates an already complex set of challenges and that scarce resources, including finances and the time of trained professionals, make it imperative that schools find ways to avoid uncoordinated or duplicated efforts. Additionally, Smylie, Lazarus, and Brownlee-Conyers (1996) found that the individual autonomy of teachers so touted as a fundamental cultural and sociological feature of the profession is *negatively* associated with student achievement, whereas accountability and organizational learning opportunities for school professionals may be the most important positive factors in improved student learning. These findings affirm the need to push toward more efforts in which teachers and other educational professionals work together (White & Wehlage, 1995, p. 23).

Within schools, differentiated professionals focus on multiple problems facing children and youth. In large schools, they routinely include classroom teachers, special education teachers, counselors, and administrators and often include full- or part-time psychologists, audiologists, speech therapists, nurses, and social workers. This complement of specialists brings more expertise and energy to bear on educational problems. At the same time, the many adult professionals in schools often work in isolation from each other, their specialties and roles having evolved to serve different aspects of the child's needs. The child is passed from professional to professional; the adults frequently do not see each other except in passing, and, with the exception of resource or special education teams who must prepare an annual Individual Educational Plan, seldom plan and work together. Each specialist may come to see the part of the child's life related to his or her specialty as the most critical to the child's well-being. Meanwhile, a child with multiple needs may receive services which compete with the finite instructional time available (Capper, 1994).

This division of labor can lead to the compartmentalization of a student's problems and school experience (see also Pounder, chapter five, this text). It can also result in subtle and not so subtle competition among professionals for control over the student's time. Yet a child upset about a family problem cannot learn. A child who cannot speak clearly has difficulty learning. A disruptive child impedes her own and others' learning. A child who spends no time on learning tasks but instead moves through a menu of supplemental services all day may understand the regimen of therapy well, but read and write poorly. Collaboration is critical among the specialists whose knowledge, skills, and caring come together to serve the whole child.

Collaboration can be defined as the cooperation of equals who voluntarily share decision making and work toward common goals. A collaborative ethic defines a set of values or principles which endorses collegial decision making and problem solving as opposed to independent action as school professionals (Friend & Cook, 1990). However, collaboration, in and of itself, does not necessarily guarantee increased efficiency, effectiveness in schooling, or empowerment of students and families (Capper, 1994, p. 273). At its best, collaboration facilitates the education of children and youth, enabling educators to have access to expanded knowledge, resources, and creative alternatives for action. In a variety of collaborative efforts, educators and researchers argue that collaboration "allows for mutual understanding and consensus, democratic decision making, and common action" (Clark et al., 1996, p.

195). It involves the understanding and participation of all parties at all stages of the work process. Assumptions about, benefits of, and barriers to collaboration among professionals can either facilitate or inhibit educational effectivensss (West, 1990).

The previous chapters in this section examined collaboration between schools and external agencies and the redesign of teachers' work toward collaborative instructional teams. This chapter focuses on the contributions and challenges of collaboration among the multiple professionals who work within the school. The roles and training of these professionals differentiate not only their responsibilities but also their orientations toward students' needs and consequently the goals, values, and priorities they pursue in their work. Thus collaboration is a very real exercise in professional compromise and tradeoffs—a process in which parents must be involved as well (Bauch & Goldring, 1995; Chubb & Moe, 1990).

Recent literature on collaboration in schools reveals an emphasis on collaboration between dyads—of professionals, constituencies, and outside agencies—and of each of these groups with parents (Sheridan, 1990). Examples of these collaborative pairings include teachers and administrators (Poole, 1995), psychologists and teachers (Duis, 1995), psychologists and social workers (Karge, 1995), and special and regular educators (Kilgore & Rubin, 1995; Welch & Sheridan, 1993). By far the majority of attention paid to school collaboration focuses on special education programs (Malekoff, Johnson, & Klappersack, 1991) or on violence and crime prevention efforts (Howard, 1994; Morris, 1992). Studies of multidisciplinary professional collaboration emphasize interagency collaboration or needed collaboration with the school psychologist (DeLeon, 1995).

Going to school should be a unified experience for children and youth, not a discrete series of consultations with independent professionals. To avoid working at cross-purposes and to maximize the synthesis and clarity of students' learning and social experiences in schools, successful collaboration among the professionals who work in schools and with parents is necessary. Multidisciplinary collaboration promotes a common language, knowledge base, and understanding of the diverse and complex challenges of teaching and learning in schools. Children face this complexity every day. So must adults. Collaborative educators need a broad understanding of one another's roles and functions and the tools of collaborative problem solving in order to maximize their positive joint impacts on children and youth toward the achievement of their goals (Welch et al., 1992).

To address the issues of intraschool professional collaboration, this chapter explores several collaboration themes: (1) professional work roles, (2) the social structure of professional work groups, (3) conflict management, and (4) collaborative problem solving. Finally, I turn to the process through which educators can work to develop collaboration among school professionals. These themes lead the reader through an analysis of the barriers to collaboration introduced above, individual and group dynamics, and the promises and pitfalls of professional collaboration. The chapter addresses the ethic and utility of collaboration that involves school professionals and parents in joint efforts to help students succeed. It also provides specific mechanisms through which educators can design collaborative problem-solving teams and utilize these professional resources in school settings.

PROFESSIONAL ROLES

A brief discussion of roles in social systems helps set the stage for this discussion of collaboration among diverse school professionals. As anyone who has ever tried to change "the way we do things around here" can testify, roles and relationships among roles become firmly imbedded in established groups. Overcoming pitfalls and achieving the promises of collaboration among professionals can be enhanced through a better understanding of their roles in schools.

Key Role Concepts and Functions

The role one holds often is a defining feature of one's identity. A work role is associated with persons who share a common professional identity and who fill a similar function in the organization. The knowledge and patterns of behavior characteristic of persons in a given work role are learned through formal education, experience, and professional and organizational socialization. Consequently, scholars and professionals talk about the process of becoming—becoming a teacher, becoming a psychologist, becoming a principal. Those who study roles often seek to understand how people come to adopt the identity of a profession as well as the knowledge and behaviors associated with it.

The central features of roles are important to this discussion of collaboration, because roles so powerfully shape people's beliefs about what is acceptable, appropriate, desirable, and *professional* behavior. A few key concepts about roles drawn from role theory will help elaborate: (1) social systems, (2) social positions, (3) behaviors, (4) expectations, (5) socialization, (6) norms, (7) values, (8) context, and (9) functions (Biddle, 1979).

First, roles exist within complex *social systems* (see also Johnson, chap. 2, Barott & Raybould, chap. 3, this text). The people within a system interact in characteristic and systematic patterns. The *social position* or role one holds determines where one fits within the system. Consequently, teachers (a social position) share characteristic and critical *behaviors* (although they may fill their roles in some unique ways) that characterize the role "teacher." Interactions among teachers and between teachers and others develop established patterns.

Second, people learn roles in a particular *context*. Other members of the system hold strong *expectations* for the role behavior of others and enforce those expectations through explicit and implicit means. New teachers, for example, learn what behaviors are expected of them in the profession (professional *socialization*) and in a particular school (organizational *socialization*). Each has powerful influence over the teacher's actions.

Third, in addition to the functions or tasks associated with a role, certain *norms* and *values* shape group expectations of someone in a role. Teachers in a school, for example, may value autonomy and privacy more than they value collaboration; the norm may be to close their classroom doors, ignoring what goes on outside the class (see also Pounder, chap. 5, Johnson chap. 2, Evans-Stout, chap. 7, this text). On the other hand, there may be a strong value for instructional coordination with grade-level team planning and shared cocurricular activities.

Professionals fulfill important *functions* in schools (see also Crow, chap. 8, this text). These functions often depend on those in other roles behaving in the expected ways so that the interactions among members of the entire group go smoothly and as expected. The theater is often used as a metaphor for this interaction of role functions. During a performance, each actor must perform her or his role in exactly the expected way so that other actors can take their cues, say their lines at the expected time (thus performing their roles), and send cues to other actors in turn. The actors are said to follow a script, to perform their roles. Actors can communicate verbally and nonverbally, signaling each other that particular milestones in the play are approaching. If anyone forgets a part or changes scripted lines, the whole cast must immediately adjust to keep the performance going.

A stellar production requires timing, knowledge of the other actors and parts, sensitivity, and quick thinking. The better the actors know each other and the other parts, the more likely they are able to adjust quickly and appropriately to the production demands. The function of each part in the play makes a great deal of difference in the success of the production. When someone forgets or alters a part, stress occurs. In social situations, role stress results when a member of the group behaves in unexpected or incongruent ways (Diamond & Allcorn, 1985; Latack, 1984). Just as actors signal each other with actions as well as words, verbal and nonverbal communication play a significant part in a group's interactions.

Finally, all these features come together in complex patterns that affect professional self-concept, work satisfaction, and work relationships. During transition and change in work roles, situational self-concepts often are reframed (Louis, 1980). Collaboration may reveal internal inconsistencies and conflicts within and among school professionals over appropriate and desired behavior (see also Evans-Stout, chap. 7, this text). Conflict may also occur over goals and priorities.

Traditional and Evolving Roles

By far the most common adult work role in schools belongs to the teacher. Illustrations of the way teachers traditionally have viewed their roles can be found in common expressions. Teachers often say, "my class," "my students," "my lesson." This speech exemplifies the established practice that a student belongs to the regular classroom schoolteacher. Yet, as we saw in Pounder's discussion of teacher work teams (chap. 5, this text), the role and function of the teacher is being redesigned and redefined as teachers seek more collaborative ways to enhance students' learning. As the traditional teacher's role changes, so do the roles of other educators and professionals within the school. New roles are added as students' require additional expertise and assistance. These new and changing roles and functions must create a holistic educational experience for students.

In this section, traditional and evolving expectations and definitions of school professional roles are introduced. The preceding discussion describing the ways roles function and interact in social systems is general and abstract in nature. However, the daily work of schools is detailed and concrete. In this section, the details—what people do and are expected to do—are discussed.

Teachers.   As the primary educators in schools, teachers are responsible for complex tasks and must respond to diverse expectations from society, parents, and their immediate work setting in the face of new and developing role expectations. As stated earlier, traditional constructs of teachers' work emphasize its complexity, autonomy, and directive features. The teacher plans, organizes, and delivers instruction. The teacher is active; the learner is passive. While this traditional view does not hold true in many teaching situations, teachers still hold themselves responsible and are held responsible by others for the organization and conduct of learning activities in school. As Smylie et al. (1996) pointed out in his restructuring research, even when many other people share decision making and influence events, the core professional is still held accountable for the outcomes. Even in the most facilitative conceptions of teaching, other education professionals are seen as support for the core work of the teacher.

Special Education Teachers. Traditionally, special education teachers were trained to provide separate, specialized, or compensatory services for students with unique needs. They provided remedial, tutorial, or behavioral interventions as well as direct, specialized instruction. Isolated, specialized programs taught by special education teachers dominated special education for many years. However, the inclusion movement is redefining the role of the special educator as students are increasingly educated within the "least restrictive environment." The role is expanding to include adjunct, consultant, or support delivery for students and teachers in the regular classroom. Other professionals in a school can voluntarily seek access to the specialist's expertise to address and resolve challenging learning and behavior problems (Johnson, Pugach, & Devlin 1990; Stainbach & Stainback, 1989). The special educator works as a colleague, a professional specialist who supports and supplements the work of the regular teacher. Special educators also are increasingly managers and coordinators of service delivery to students who need instructional support rather than treatment.

Psychologist. Testing comes to mind when most people think of the school psychologist. With the increase of students diagnosed as disabled, at risk of failure, or having special needs, many school psychologists spend most of their time administering individual standardized tests, consulting with parents and teachers, or providing psychological services (Gutkin & Conoley, 1990). Most broadly, school psychologists define their work as applying knowledge from the psychology discipline to the education problems of children (Siegel & Colke, 1990). Ideally, they can function as consultants or members of intervention assistance teams, bringing knowledge about learning concepts, child development, intellectual and social functioning, child and family relations, problem solving, and, in some cases, organizational development. Some use the term *intervention* to describe the entry of a school psychologist into the learning setting—intervening into a full-blown crisis—and see the psychologist's role beginning when student learning problems become unmanageable.

Principal. Principals exert formal and informal influence over the work of teachers through traditional authority as well a various forms of transformational, inspirational, visionary, or instructional leadership. Principals' formal authority over resources and rewards, accepted power to act for the group, and expected leadership in team and group work efforts make them influential members of schools. Although vigorous debate surrounds the best or most appropriate role of the principal as formal leader of a school, the principal's support for change, development, or stability is recognized as a critical factor in school success. Lists of principals' roles and functions become exhausting to read if not exhaustive—administrator, coordinator, decision maker, instructional leader, policymaker, delegator, public relations manager, curriculum planner, climate manager, supervisor, evaluator, enforcer, disciplinarian.

Counselor.   School counselors ground their work in the discipline of psychology. While some are licensed counseling social workers, most state certification requirements continue to emphasize an educational psychology background for school counselors. The present range of counselor functions is daunting: individual and group counseling, assessment (particularly as related to educational and career decisions), student academic planning, course scheduling, and student, parent, or faculty consultation, and training or organizational development. Counseling services can be academic, vocational, psychological, and/or personal. Counselors often conceive of their role as a child advocate or human development specialist—facilitating an ongoing process rather than fixing something that is broken. With their professional roots in psychology, counselors' and school psychologists' role conceptions often overlap (e.g., child advocate, counselor, student, parent, or faculty consultant).

Social Worker.   Increasingly, schools are including social workers among the school personnel. The social worker takes responsibility for students' interactions and relationships with their primary social support groups—parents, families, friends, community. Social workers often concentrate their efforts on family relationships, social problems in the community, support groups, and community services. The roles and functions of counselors, psychologists, and social workers seem distinct in their formal disciplines; in schools, the roles may overlap, even compete. Often social work services are provided by agencies outside the school, leading to interagency services like those discussed by Galvin (chapter four, this text). In some community collaboratives, the school social worker is the professional representative of the school to larger agency collaboratives (Capper, 1994; Keith, 1996).

It can be an interesting exercise to ask educators what their beliefs are about the roles and functions of principals, counselors, psychologists, special educators, and social workers. Figure 6.1 emerged from just such an activity in a graduate course for educators on multiprofessional collaboration (see also Matthews, chap. 9, this text).

FIGURE 6.1
Educator Roles and Functions

Principal

Role: Administrator and coordinator, manager, decision maker, instructional leader, coordinator, policy maker, implementor, disseminator, leader, boss, educational leader, delegator (assignments and authority), team member, public relations officer and community liaison, enforcer, evaluator, special education liaison officer

Functions: Supervise and support faculty; oversee public relations; coordinate community relations, prepare and supervise budget and finance; implement state and district policies and board goals; supervise physical facilities; coordinate administrative staff; organize and lead faculty meetings; make, control, and organize decisions; purchase and acquire materials; discipline students; evaluate; coordinate; prepare the school schedule and calendar; hire staff and faculty; set school goals; coordinate special and regular education

Counselor

Role: Guide; student career counselor; faculty supporter; advisor; student course scheduler, student supporter and advocate, academic (standardized) test administrator, child-study team member, liaison among students, parents, and teachers; post secondary education consultant; problem-solver

Functions: Conduct and evaluate tests (academic, interest, aptitude); schedule students' courses; advocate in behalf of students; support faculty; serve as family-school intermediary; conduct group and individual counseling (emotional, social, preventative); conduct preventative, social skills, and other general student-oriented programs; provide vocational and career guidance; conduct graduation audits; advise students on scholarships and financial aid; serve as a liaison and intermediary between faculty and students; provide referrals to appropriate agencies

School Psychologist

Role: Behavioral evaluator; behavioral and psychological therapist; test administrator (psychological and instructional assessment); guidance counselor; consultant; helper; interdisciplinary team member (i.e., special education); diagnostician; intervention planner; classroom consultant

Functions: Recommend student placement; conduct and evaluate tests; provide behavioral, psychological and emotional counseling; provide

(continued on next page

FIGURE 6.1 *(continued)*

mentoring support for instructional and resource teams; provide behavioral management support; attend Individual Educational Plan meetings; conduct conflict resolution; provide intervention, evaluation, and placement support; provide student individual and group counseling; supervise student peer counselors; coordinate services with outside agencies and resources

Teacher

Role: Teacher; teacher of the basic or core curriculum; facilitator for learning; reference provider for special and support services; implementer of school policy; curriculum designer; designer and assessor of learning strategies; evaluator; classroom manager; role model; team member; disciplinarian; tester; provider of love and support; arbitrator; counselor; motivator

Functions: Impart information; train students in self discipline; classroom management; educational planning; love and support; design, apply, and choose curriculum; arbitrate; create a learning environment; implement state and district policy; measure and assess learning and student progress; test; keep attendance records; supervise recess, bus, and lunchroom; conduct parent conferences; provide liaison and public relations services; record keeping; give student grades; be a role model; help students apply knowledge to situations; coordinate student tasks; attend conventions and special meetings; participate in support team activities; recognize and refer problems; supervise and support clubs and extra curricular activities; photocopying

The lack of agreement, omissions, and overlapping responsibilities in this educator-generated list illustrate that, while clear conceptual views of educator roles exist, in this case the devil is in the details. Collaborative efforts within schools face ambiguous and overlapping beliefs and practices about appropriate educator roles, functions, and areas of expertise. One way to understand how the professionals in a particular school view their roles and relationships is to ask them to construct similar lists as individuals—identifying what they actually do in their present roles and then sharing and discussing their respective lists. The discussion that followed the compilation of the list in figure 6.1 was vigorous and, at times, frustrating to educators who felt that their colleagues simply "did not understand" their roles. This misunderstanding or honest disagreement can be rooted in a long work history.

THE SOCIAL STRUCTURE OF
PROFESSIONAL WORK GROUPS

The social structure of a school, its social system, creates the interpretations people draw from "objective" work features. The social structure shapes perceptions about what is good and right and about the usefulness and desirability of collaboration. It is difficult for people who are experiencing the effects of social structure on collaboration to "pin down" those effects, because social structure is both a very real and powerful part of professional work and an abstract concept. Its abstraction makes many of its impacts seem like fantastic fancy, like painting a portrait of air, especially when purely "rational" job descriptions, lists of goals, and organizational charts delineating task responsibilities seem so much more "real." Like air, however, a social system can make its effects felt.

A school's social structure consists of the people who work and study as well as their patterns of behavior and relationships with each other (see also Johnson, chap. 2, and Barott & Raybould, chap. 3, this text). Researchers have found that factors shaping this social system include: organizational resources; norms, values, and expectations; intraorganizational politics and power; perceptions of work and of role routinization and clarity; inertia; and leadership (Johnson, 1990a). Each of these factors deserves brief elaboration.

Organizational *resources* constitute the most visible factor shaping the school social system. Resources can provide strong incentives for and support for collaboration, but their scarcity also can limit collaborative activity and impacts (Mitchell, 1986). Resources found most likely to affect collaboration include: information, materials, clients, budget, human support services, training or knowledge, time, work environment and space, tools and equipment, and authority (Hart, 1990b). Information, for example, empowers those who possess it. In a school where one person or privileged group controls access to important information (e.g., students' academic records, the supplies and textbook budgets, planned building renovations, the political beliefs and goals of the PTA president), others who are denied information access do not bring the same strength to a potential collaboration (see also Crow, chap. 8, for a discussion of balance of power, influence, etc.). Time has the same impact. If one group has substantial discretionary control over how professional time is allocated and another has little or no time discretion, collaborative interactions are imbalanced. For each of these resources, one can imagine many examples of their favorable or unfavorable impact on the social structure of a collaborative environment.

The *norms, values, and expectations* of the group (and of individual

roles, as emphasized in the earlier discussion) exert another strong influence over the form and outcomes of collaboration. For example, if there
is a norm that teachers arrive fifteen minutes before school starts and
leave within an hour after school ends, then teachers who come too
early and stay too late often are criticized for making others look bad
(Hart, 1987). They have violated a norm; in union parlance, they are
rate busters. Is there an expectation that teachers, counselors, psychologists, and social workers attend a weekly team meeting to discuss difficult student problems at the grade, department, or school level? If so,
then the group can exert tremendous pressure on a professional colleague who frequently schedules competing appointments or offers
other excuses for regularly missing team meetings. Is each teacher's
classroom a "kingdom," a private space into which others may venture
only with permission and to which the door is usually closed? If the
"real" work of teachers is making classroom presentations and administering tests; then a teacher might plead to be left alone to do what he
or she is "paid to do." Each reader can undoubtedly think of similar
examples from schools in which he or she has worked that would affect
professional collaboration within a school.

An ethic or norm of collaboration, identified earlier in this chapter,
is a critical component of collaborative decision making and professional work in schools (Welch, et al., 1992). To promote a collaborative
school social structure, collaborative norms, values, and expectations
will require development and nurturing. Fortunately, schools are not
monolithic, identical social systems and social structures can be influenced and changed. Despite studies on the sociology of teaching (Johnson, 1990a, 1990b: Lortie, 1975; Waller, 1933) describing a profession
in which civility, equality, and privacy dominate rules of interaction,
evidence exists that significant differences may be rooted in work subgroups such as grade-level teams, special education units, or identifiable
sections of the school—"the west hall group" (Hart, 1990a; Smylie et
al., 1996). Also, professionals' ability to see their work differently can
be influenced by different forms of social interaction such as their position in an organization's central communication network or involvement with outsiders (Dean & Brass, 1985). This research suggests that
there are ways to influence the collaborative norm or ethic of a school.

A third aspect of work group social structure affecting collaboration
is *intraorganizational politics and power*. Who is aligned with whom?
Who negotiates with, has power over, or influences whom? For example, in one school in which I worked, the wood shop teacher consistently
overspent his materials budget by a few thousand dollars each year. The
principal covered the overrun out of general textbook and supplies
accounts. Each year, department heads met to evaluate and plan the

next year's budgets (participative decision-making), but only the formal proposed budgets were shared such that none of the other heads realized that their colleague had an "understanding" with the principal that he would look the other way when budgeted funds were overspent. Bacharach, Bamberger, and Conley (1990) point out that the reality of organizations as negotiated political systems affect school people's perceptions of their personal and professional power. The principal's tacit spending agreement effectively gave the wood shop teacher access to resources outside the established decision making structure, resources that were unavailable to others. Administrative mandates, the needs and demands of parents, the influence of special interest groups, and a multitude of other demands are tacitly negotiated among administrators, teachers, community members, and the other professionals who work in schools. The effects of this micropolitical reality of power relationships, coalitions, and bargaining affects the real work outcomes of collaboration, in addition to affecting the dynamics of the collaborative effort itself (Bacharach & Mundell, 1993). Even such factors as the relative status of each educator's professional group within the larger community (i.e., psychologist versus teacher versus counselor versus principal) affect the level of micropolitical influence one might have.

A fourth aspect of schools as social work groups springs from *features* of the work place such as supervision, routinization, and ambiguity. A group of teachers or psychologists might find particular features of their work (e.g., shared space, the privacy of the traditional classroom, interdependence of teacher teams) to be more or less satisfying and legitimate. So, to increase the amount and influence of collaboration one must diagnose and assess how the features of new collaborative work relationships might be greeted within a school. What existing work place features could be modified to become more satisfying and which ones should be left undisturbed? Knowledge about the existing school work features allows those seeking to enhance collaboration to make adjustments and influence established values (Conley, Bacharach & Bauer, 1989; Chubb, 1988; Chubb & Moe, 1988). Among the strongest considerations are "institutionalized expectations about the nature of education . . . and the entrenched roles of education participants" (Angus, 1988, p. 30), including all the items in the long lists of roles and functions found in figure 6.1 (or the reader's own lists).

Fifth, organizational *inertia or resilience* affects changes necessary to create more collaborative work (see also Barott & Raybould, chap. 3, this text). How many times have those seeking a change been greeted with, "We've always done it this way," or "We don't do things that way around here"? Brief and Downey (1983) showed that even "wrong" views about work organization can be resilient and long lasting. They concluded from their research that even if people's norms, expectations, and beliefs are useful only as "social glue," it does not mean that they will easily be replaced. In some cases, threat and stress make people more determined to preserve their social structure and traditions. For example, if educators feel that they are being pressured to collaborate—under attack from an embattled political environment—inertia and resistance to collaboration may increase, even in the face of objective arguments that collaboration will better achieve educational goals. In this tendency, educators are no different than other people.

Finally, *leadership* plays an important part in valuing and structuring the opportunities and changes needed to develop a more collaborative professional work structure in schools. While an exaggerated emphasis on the heroic power of formal leadership positions is always risky, researchers find that leaders play a significant part in making major changes possible in education and other organizations. According to Chubb (1988, p. 33), leadership in high-performing schools is "more pedagogical and less managerial." It is also stronger, more forceful, and retains a focus on communication and the pursuit of vision. Decision making is more democratic and relationships between teachers and principals more cooperative, and Chubb emphasizes the importance of school-level autonomy. Collaboration may require school leaders to evaluate tasks, not individuals, as groups work together under the assurance that the collaborative effort and each participant's contribution to its effectiveness is the focus of the evaluation and assessment. This is particularly important in a school transitioning to a more collaborative social structure, where teachers and others are reluctant to take on a new structure that might hold them personally accountable for outcomes when they have lost individual control over processes (see also Pounder, chap. 5, this text).

Because teachers are the most numerous and traditionally powerful professionals working in schools, teachers' values about work features strongly affect attitudes toward collaborative work structures among other school professionals. The values of the other professionals involved in these collaboratives also will be important. Hart (1994b) found that valued features of work differ substantially among teachers, who are far from a monolithic group sharing homogenous work values. In each school, the constellation of professionals and their personal as well as professional characteristics must be considered.

In the preceding discussion, the reader may be struck by the absence of a concrete examination of the actual social structures and features of work in a school—what people do every day. *Each and every school* will have a unique blend of generally held views, idiosyncrasies, resources, and other social structure features and must assess and respond to this unique mix. Rather than isolating one system and describing it, I would challenge each school desiring to construct a more collaborative work structure to assess and understand its unique social structure. When combined with the technical requirements of the work, the socio technical design of work discussed below can influence the degree and impact of school collaboration.

Sociotechnical Design

In the lists of educator roles and functions compiled in figure 6.1, one can see how the functions a particular person fulfills may overlap with the functions of others and, conversely, that each professional role includes some very clear, core, and unique features. One research tradition, sociotechnical work design, helps elucidate how these roles and functions together with organizational social structure can be better understood and used to enhance intragroup collaboration in schools. This tradition specifically emphasizes, in concert, the social (as previously discussed) and the technical requirements of the work done (Cherns, 1987; Trist, 1981). The processes by which work technology and social structure affect people's performance and satisfaction require constant reconsideration (Jones, 1984). One scholar pointed out that "the most effective organizations will be those in which the technology and the organization structure and social processes are designed to fit together" (Whyte, 1991, p. 97).

Sociotechnical design emphasizes a number of fundamental principles. First among these principles, the social and technical features of the work must be compatible. Additionally, administrators should: (1) limit specifications about how people must do their work; (2) allow many supervisory functions to be distributed; (3) facilitate the free flow of information, knowledge, and learning; and (4) provide access to resources and the authority to use them. The system should guard against a "firefighting" mentality and structure of work, promote integration, and provide for adjustment periods during major transitions. Finally, one should always consider both social and technical issues when supporting or redesigning work (Chern, 1987). Research in schools supports the authenticity of these principles for school work design (Hart, 1990a, 1992, 1994a, 1994b; Smylie 1994).

The primary work technologies or work structures of principals, counselors, social workers, special educators, audiologists, and therapists differ substantially in tradition and may openly conflict during collaboration. Additionally, as was noted previously, these professions have developed within isolated, discrete environments that infrequently require them to work collaboratively outside their groups (or even within their groups). To promote more collaborative work among these professionals, sociotechnical work design suggests some specific steps for developing and implementing collaborative work environments: (1) Avoid overspecification of ways in which collaboration should play out in each school; (2) protect collaboration from other aspects of the school based on different assumptions and methods; (3) share information, knowledge, and learning among all those involved and encourage the free flow of information about the collaborative work arrangements in the community; (4) make necessary adjustments to the school (such as scheduling) to accommodate the innovation; and, perhaps most importantly; (5) provide for the development of a transition organization, acknowledge its unique stage in the overall implementation, and be tolerant and supportive of the pressures that are unique to the transition period (Hart, 1995).

However, a caution is offered. Manipulating collaborative and participatory work structures as a means of control is a major mistake.

> [T]hose who feel excluded or disenfranchised may see participation as a way of gaining some control over a host of decisions affecting their lives, or indeed, they may refuse participation if they do not believe there are prospects for such gains; obversely, those in positions of power may view participation as a tool to secure subordinates' compliance with administrative decisions, commitment to management goals, assistance in the performance of management functions, or simply, to improve productivity. (Keith, 1996, p. 49)

Rather, authenticity is an important part of the process of sociotechnical design, not just increased productivity or other less obvious agendas. Collaborative teams must balance their social and technical features to better achieve their shared goals for students' education.

> [P]articipation must be extended beyond teachers to include students and the local community . . . [F]irst, because one of the crucial factors in urban school failure is the sociocultural distance between students' and teachers' worlds; and second, because system change requires the empowerment of the community. (Keith, 1996, p. 48)

Collaborative Teams

The team is the dominant metaphor for collaborative groups. A fundamental issue must regularly be faced by members of collaborative teams—the power of one versus the summative or perhaps synergistic power of the whole. In this section, teams and effective teaming are examined by drawing upon perspectives from counseling and organizational development. Specific examples of collaborative teaming in schools can be found in other chapters.

Teams draw on the strengths of their different members while openly acknowledging, even celebrating, positive interdependence. However, many educators assume that a team is automatically made up of totally equal peers possessing identical talents and responsibilities (Maeroff, 1993). Others see teaming and leadership as mutually exclusive, perhaps even contradictory (Muncey & McQuillan, 1996), and identify paradoxes arising from teaming endeavors (Pounder, 1995). Consequently, multidisciplinary teams in education face an immediate challenge—distinguishing between autonomy and isolation so that interdependence does not contradict professional autonomy but reduces isolation (see also Johnson, chap. 2, Pounder, chap. 5, and Evans-Stout, chap. 7, this text).

Recent research on collaborative work designs in schools emphasizes the importance of making this distinction. Smylie et al. (1996) found in their analysis of longitudinal data that work group autonomy—conceptualized as control by the team over the resources and work structures necessary to do the work and accountability for its outcomes—was positively associated with student achievement, whereas *individual teacher autonomy* conceptualized more traditionally was *negatively* associated with student achievement. These are the first long-term research results on a large data set that lay out the costs of retaining noncollaborative work features.

A counseling perspective on effective teams offers an explicit view of what multidisciplinary collaborative teaming might look like in education. This perspective relies on ideals of effective team work, including essential elements of *positive interdependence, individual accountability, face to face interaction, collaborative skills,* and *group processes* (Johnson & Johnson, 1987).

As pointed out above, *positive interdependence* is not a contradiction to professional autonomy. Rather it links group members through mutually beneficial contributions from each. These contributions enhance each member's and the group's success. The traditional perspective on professional autonomy for educators views interdependence skeptically, seeing it as a barrier to individual goal setting, roles, tasks, rewards, and use of resources.

Individual accountability for productive participation in and contributions to the team can help alleviate resistance to interdependence while protecting educators from excessive isolation frequently labeled "professional autonomy." Team members not only are interdependent but can identify and analyze the critical contributions each professional brings to the work of the team. Openness and responsiveness to the expertise and perspective of each multidisciplinary team member enhances problem solving and the team interaction process, and it takes maximum advantage of each member of the group (Welch et al., 1992).

Another important aspect of team work involves *face to face interaction* (Welch et al., 1992) or technologically enhanced interaction that recreates the intimacy and interaction levels previously available only through face-to-face meetings (Schrage, 1990). Many different approaches to interaction processes are employed by those seeking to enhance the effectiveness of teams—from interpersonal communication styles perspectives to Myers-Briggs personality inventories.

Finally, many seeking to promote the increased use of teams in educational problem solving argue that a new approach to professional work that develops *collaborative skills, attitudes,* and *processes* is required. There is an element of irony to this approach: effective problem solving may occur because of, rather than in spite of, team members' differences in professional orientations. A counseling psychology approach such as the one just discussed might emphasize member cohesion, trust, openness, and norm building (Welch et al., 1992). An alternative approach might suggest that innovative, creative problem solving must draw upon the productive use of team conflict and disagreement, rejecting commitments to consensus building (Herman, 1994; Schrage, 1990).

As the reader can see from this brief introduction, team building immediately comes up against the social dynamics of a multidisciplinary system with strong professional norms as well as organizational or school norms (Bidwell & Vreeland, 1977). Tapping the power of these groups requires a clear understanding of the sincere and deeply felt professional differences of group members and the establishment of unique interaction processes for each and every team.

Many writers in organizational behavior and organizational development question the overuse of the team metaphor, although education teams lack the competitive tone of the sports metaphor that appears in business literature. Collaboration, according to some new perspectives, must move beyond the team metaphor, because so many preconceptions and competitive images burden generally held concepts of teams (Schrage, 1990). For example, most people expect a team to have a captain, and they expect that captain to be the administrator. Working as a member of a collaborative faculty team, my colleagues and I noticed that these expectations are so firmly imbedded that our educator students consistently expected the person role-playing the administrator part in collaboration exercises to assume the leadership responsibilities. Specifically, in group exercises, students playing the administrator role typically took over as "team leader" and if they did not do so immediately, members of the group pressured them to do so (Welch et al., 1992). Writers such as Schrage (1990) argue that, to combat this deeply imbedded expectation and realize collaboration's full potential, we must abandon team metaphors and master the dynamics of creative collaboration. Schrage illustrates this need with a story: At a job interview, a friend was asked if he was a team player. "Yes," he replied, "team captain" (p. xi). Schrage argues that collaboration is an act of shared discovery and creation—needed when one person's charm, charisma, authority, or expertise is insufficient to the task at hand. The complex problems faced by modern educators frequently fit this situation. They require the specialties that have sprung up in response to the complexity of school work problems, but they require that these specialists marshal their forces in creative and innovative ways.

A caution is in order. As with any construct, any extreme form can be dysfunctional. Collaboration, teams, collegiality, group process, and consensus are not universally salutary. Herman (1994) cautions that cooperative, conciliatory terms can create pressure for conformity—the groupthink mentality that Janis (1982) warned us about so persuasively. Collaborative work teams consistently must balance the creativity of the individual and the power of the group, guarding against the suppression of important ideas under the guise of cohesiveness and consensus. Conflict thus is both a challenge and a useful tool for effective collaborative teams.

CONFLICT MANAGEMENT

As differing professional norms come together within a collaborative school work group, conflict can arise (see also Barott & Raybould, chap. 3, this text). Different perspectives of conflict suggest different approaches to managing conflict. One view categorizes conflict as personal or impersonal and views conflict avoidance or resolution as very important. An example of this approach is offered by Welch et al. (1992):

> Both personal (e.g., belonging, control, personality, involvement) and impersonal (e.g., time, energy, task, information) sources of conflict [exist] . . . Effective ways of avoiding conflicts [are] . . . (1) avoiding arguing for one's own judgments, (2) changing one's mind simply to avoid conflict and promote harmony, (3) avoiding conflict-reducing techniques, and (4) not perceiving differences of opinion as detrimental. (p.13)

This perspective characterizes controversies as destructive or constructive depending on the processes by which they are managed and by their outcome. Constructive controversy is defined as a problem, whereas destructive controversy is defined as a win-lose situation. From this perspective, cohesion and positive relationships among members promote constructive outcomes.

Other perspectives on conflict assert that this approach focuses too directly on group cohesion and insufficiently on the poorly established link between group satisfaction and performance. Conflict management is a more useful approach (Mayer, 1995). From this point of view, conflicting interests and behavior are separate dimensions, and serious conflicts of interest arise legitimately within organizations, particularly at organizational interfaces (such as the interface between teacher, psychologist, and social worker). Brown (1983, p. 15) emphasizes this characteristic: "The more numerous and diverse the levels and specialized divisions within an organization, the more opportunities for conflict at the interfaces." At the same time, he reminds us that "The more interdependence between parties, the higher the cost of poorly managed conflict at their interface." Finally, the social differences among those at the interface make "authority, responsibility, and appropriate behavior" often unclear. Timeliness in dealing with these conflicts at the interface is critical (see also Pounder, chap. 5, this text)." [A] key to effective conflict management, to keeping relationships vital and preventing destructive conflicts, is to *confront every issue now* (or as close to"now" as possible). *Do not avoid them"* (Mayer, 1995, p. 46).

Power is missing from many educators' views of conflict—power to prevail, to control, to set goals, to secure resources—in large part because it violates a work culture norm of cordiality and equality. Fights, threats, and aggression are a reality in organizational life that educators may downplay and consequently handle poorly. Additionally, educators may fail to recognize that some people enjoy conflict (as a game, a debate) or use it to achieve the "imposition of truth" (Ogley, 1991, p. 148).

However, for professionals in schools, most conflicts do not reach the level of crisis or intensity that many conflict analysts describe. What is more common is latent, ongoing conflict that results in resistance and obstruction rather than overt confrontation. Balanced power relationships, involvement of key players, realistic deadlines, and framing debates that do not focus on sacrosanct values still are important as educators work to manage and resolve conflict among members of collaborative professional teams (Susskind & Cruikshank, 1987). Weeks (1992) lays out eight essential steps to effective conflict resolution that differ from the relational emphasis seen in counseling approaches. They are: (1) create an effective atmosphere through personal preparation, timing, a context that promotes connected rather than embattled positions; (2) clarify perceptions of the basis and nature of the conflict (values, means, ends, self-perceptions, power,"winning," etc.); (3) focus on individual and shared needs; (4) build shared positive power that does *not* disempower others, nor focus on attempts to gain advantage over others, nor focus on power over rather than power with, nor win-lose constructs; (5)

look to the future, and learn from the past; (6) generate options; (7) develop action steps; and (8) make mutual-benefit agreements.

As one can see, these approaches must be tailor-made for specific team situations. The combination of context, specific problems to be addressed, mix of professional and personal expertise and features, and nature of the culture and community will shape conflict resolution and conflict management in collaborative teams. If groups emphasize the power *to* achieve their goals rather than the power *over* others, they will have moved a long way toward tapping the salutary effects of all approaches to conflict management in collaborative teams.

In figure 6.2, the types of conflict, some decision strategies for managing conflict, the functions and dysfunctions, and constructive and destructive conflict processes are summarized. Team members can use this table as a reference to check their reactions to conflict and to analyze the salutary and dysfunctional aspects of conflict in multi-disciplinary teams. While attending to conflict and its functions, however, the principal goal of collaborative teams is effective problem solving.

COLLABORATIVE PROBLEM SOLVING

The preceding discussion suggests that a healthy and productive collaborative structure for solving education problems has two features that must be monitored for a salutary and appropriate balance: (1) the ability to work with others whose professional orientation, talents, and knowledge differ and (2) the ability to take maximum advantage of the different professional orientations, talents, and knowledge of the individuals in the group.

A general problem-solving model always is helpful for a collaborative team (see also Matthews, chap. 9, this text). One approach drawn from work by Bergan and Dratochwill (1990), Conley et al. (1989), and Zins, Curtis, Graden, and Ponti (1988) has been found to be useful in education settings—both in training and in practice. This approach allows a group to progress from initial problem determination and clarification to brainstorming and choosing among solution alternatives, to development and evaluation of a strategy or action plan. While it is excessively *rational* in the sense that it simplifies the many iterations and feedback loops through which the process progresses, it is a useful tool in assessing movement through problem solving stages.

The first step, *problem identification,* may be very formal (a referral from a teacher or parent; a crisis or precipitating event), or it may result from a gradually increasing awareness that something is amiss and intervention is required. Naming a problem is a very significant step, because

FIGURE 6.2
Conflict Types, Strategies, and Functions

Types of Conflict

Realistic Conflict—means and ends are opposed, differences in values and interests
Nonrealistic Conflict—releases tension, deflected hostility, historical tradition
Institutionalized Conflict—rules, predictable behavior, continuity
Primary Conflict—face-to-face
Mediated Conflict—indirect, not face-to-face
Personal and subjective as opposed to impersonal (but not necessarily object)
Conflicts of Right (agreed upon standards or over what standard are appropriate)
Conflicts of Interest (new standards, changes in standards, differential benefits)

Decision Strategies for Managing Conflict

- Know the variables necessary to understand conflict processes and outcomes: organizational properties of the interacting units, conflicts of interest, role expectations, personality and other predispositions of individuals, external conflict-regulating norms, rules, and procedures, previous conflict interaction.
- Learn strategies for reducing the perception of conflict: give up conflicting interest, focus on alternatives to conflict
- Learn strategies for managing conflict through information processing: acquire information about own and others' outcomes, identify and utilize social motives, implement actions that maximize the minimum payoff, generate conflicting opinions, prepare position papers
- Manage conflict through joint agreements: bring in a disinterested third part, mutually adjust, form stable coalition, form minimum winning size coalition, collude or merge
- Manage conflict through structural mechanisms: redefine conflict situation, use market mechanisms, restructure the environment, appeal to legal system, issue directives, mediate and arbitrate, vote, trade-off support (Adapted from Kenneth R. MacCrimmon, Ronald N. Taylor)

Functions of Conflict

- Set group boundaries, strengthen cohesiveness and separateness
- Reduces tension if dealt with and permits social interaction under stress
- Helps clarify objectives
- Establish group norms
- Without conflict, relations result in subordination rather than agreement
- Encourages group norms
- Without conflict, relations result in subordination rather than agreement
- Encourages collaboration and division of labor.

(continued on next page)

FIGURE 6.2 *(continued)*

Positive Effects of Conflict

- Increases liking
- Increases individual involvement
- Provides an outlet for hostility
- Is a stimulus for critical feeling and feedback
- Can facilitate consensus development
- (Conflict can be damaging if it threatens the identity of the team. The groups' success should be measured by quality of decision rather than the efficiency of time.)

Sources of Conflict

- Impersonal: time, resources, space/physical, understanding the problem, cliches
- Personal: involvement, belonging, control, affection, roles-own conception, task (affective response), rewards (intrinsic and extrinsic), personality, self interest, subgroups and interests, external loyalties

Constructive and destructive conflicts: Determined on the basis of the processes by which they are managed and on their outcomes

Constructive	Destructive
Defining the controversy as a problem	Defining the controversy as a win-lose situation
Participation by all group members	Participation by only a few group members; self-censorship and withdrawal
Open and honest expression of ideas and feelings	Closed or deceitful expression of ideas and feelings
Everyone's contributions listened to, given attention, taken seriously, valued, and respected	The contributions of many members ignored, devalued, not respected, and treated lightly
Quiet members encouraged to participate	Quiet members not encouraged to participate
Effective sending and receiving— Communication skill used	Communication skills not used
Differences in opinions and ideas sought out and clarified	Differences in opinions and ideas ignored or suppressed
Underlying assumptions and frames of references brought out into the open and discussed	Underlying assumptions and frames of references not brought out into the open and discussed

(continued on next page)

FIGURE 6.2 *(continued)*

Constructive	Destructive
Disagreement not taken as personal rejection by some or all group members	Disagreement taken as personal rejection by some or all group members
Adequate differentiation of positions; differences clearly understood	Inadequate differentiation of positions; differences not clearly understood
Adequate integration of positions; similarities clearly understood and positions combined in creative synthesis	Inadequate integration of positions; similarities not clearly understood and positions not combined in creative synthesis
Emotions responded to with involvement and other emotions	Emotions responded to by uninvolved understanding or ignored
Equal situational power among all members	Unequal power among group members
Moderate level of tensions	Tension level too low or too high for productive problem solving
Incentives present for creative resolutions	Incentives present for domination and winning
A mutually satisfying solution worked for and arrived at	Conflict-reducing procedures; tossing a coin, voting, negotiation used

Outcomes

Constructive	Destructive
Decisions of high quality	Decisions of low quality
High creativity of decision	Low creativity of decision
Members feel understood and listened to	Members feel misunderstood or ignored
Members feel responsible and committed to group decision	Some or all members feel no responsibility for, or commitment to, the decision
Members highly satisfied with the decision, their participation, and the process of the work group	Members highly dissatisfied with the decision, their participation, and the process of group work
Cohesion and member liking for one another is high	Cohesion and member liking for one another is low
Members feel accepted and liked by other group members	Members feel rejected and disliked by other group members
High level of trust among members	Low level of trust among members

(continued on next page)

FIGURE 6.2 *(continued)*

Constructive	Destructive
Feelings released and dissipated; tension decreased; positive feelings dominant	Feelings repressed, suppressed, and still present; tension increased, negative feelings dominant
Ability to mange controversy increased	Ability to manage controversy decreased
High level of learning about the issues under discussion	Low level of learning about the issues under discussion

naming and framing often draw boundaries around and focus the direction of subsequent steps. Next, the group engages in *problem analysis* (nature, frequency, duration, setting). *Brainstorming* possible solutions follows, along with ongoing *information gathering*.

Next the group *evaluates potential actions/solutions* and chooses those they believe are the best, winnowing down the choices until an action decision is reached. The next step is to *develop a plan*, specifying the *responsibilities of each member* and the *time frame* in which actions are taken and the outcomes expected. The *implementation* of the plan follows, along with ongoing *assessment* of the outcomes. If the implementation is, in the judgment of the group, unsuccessful, the process begins again. If successful, the implementation process is continued.

A caution is in order. The bounded rationality of human cognition and the impossibility of surveying all possible solutions and choosing the "best" alternative because of that bounded rationality and of practical limits on available information make problem solving far more complex than this rather simple process might imply. Additionally, the value conflicts and differing professional norms of group members will lead to sincere and sometime serious differences over the most important aspects of a given problem, the most pressing goals the group should pursue, and the desired outcomes. Within these limitations, collaborative problem solving can move forward with the aid of a clearly understood problem solving process.

DEVELOPING COLLABORATION
AMONG SCHOOL PROFESSIONALS

Implicit in this chapter is the idea that consultation is more than professionals sharing knowledge with one another; collaboration involves mutual effort among professionals and parents to meet the needs of children and youth (Thomas et al., 1995). Students attend schools, rather than consulting with each school-based professional in an individual client-professional relationship. Students' educational successes are in the hands of the school rather than of its teachers, administrators, psychologists, and counselors as individuals. The professionals who work in schools must function very differently than they would where the norms and goals of their profession alone structured their work with students (Bidwell and Vreeland, 1977). Thus, schools must structure the work of its professional members to provide a holistic and effective educational experience for its students. The following discussion turns to some processes, exercises, and evaluation techniques educators can use to enhance the quality and impacts of professional collaboration in their school settings.

Collaborative work arrangements are likely to create pressures for school professionals due to the comprehensive nature of work changes that affect fundamental role experiences. Schools can help work group members address their changing professional roles and functions. You might recall from the discussion of role theory with which the chapter began that specific roles and functions, behaviors, cultural norms, beliefs, expectations, and perceptions affect professionals' work roles. Role stress in the form of role conflict, role ambiguity, and role overload can affect people's ability to do their best work. Figure 6.3 provides an exercise based on these precepts of role theory that can be used in any school setting to understand and articulate the implications of a collaborative work group initiative for professionals' roles.

Another way in which schools can promote the success of collaborative professional work groups is to spend some time assessing the team work process. While one of the acknowledged pitfalls of collaboration is a too-intensive focus on group interactions at the expense of group goals and tasks, an equivalent danger lurks at the other extreme: that time will be wasted in dysfunctional conflict because insufficient attention is paid to the team's interaction processes.

Figure 6.4 presents another simple evaluation exercise for a collaborative team. Five aspects or dimensions of effective teams are laid out. Teams can use several techniques for self-evaluation. One method is for each member of the team to be asked periodically to evaluate a recently completed team task or project, analyzing each of the dimensions of task orientation, role clarification, communication and collaboration, participation of group members, and conflict management.

Another method requires a little advanced planning and a bit more risk taking, but it is very revealing. The collaborative team can have several of its sessions videotaped. Members then can review the videotapes together or individually and assess the team on dimensions listed in figure 6.4 or other important criteria. Outcomes of this evaluation process

FIGURE 6.3
Role Theory Exercise

Role:	Discuss/list examples of traditional and changing roles for teacher, special educator, counselor, psychologist, social worker, principal, parent
Role description:	Discuss/list examples of specific behaviors of traditional and changing roles for each of these groups
Role prescription:	Discuss/list and compare and contrast traditional and changing cultural norms and beliefs regarding the roles filled by the role encumbants in your school
Role expectation:	Discuss/list and compare and contrast traditional and changing expectations of roles for each of these groups
Role perception:	Compare and contrast changing role perceptions for each of these groups
Role conflict:	Identify/list examples of actual and potential role conflict in change processes associated with collaboration and teaming
Role ambiguity:	Identify/list examples of actual and potential ambiguities associated with roles in teaming
Role overload:	Identify/list examples of actual and potential overload associated with roles in teaming

For each of the preceding issues, identify differences in perceptions and expectations that exist among the important groups that need to collaborate in your school (e.g., parents, teachers, psychologists, principals. What differences will affect collaborative work? How will you confront and address these differences?).

can include: (1) individual and private assessments of one's own contribution and performance, (2) private assessments of the team's processes, (3) private assessments of the outcome or goal accomplishment of the team, and (4) team assessments of its function and outcomes as part of a team-building exercise. Members can evaluate areas such as role integrity (content/expertise), role flexibility, contributions to team processing, responsiveness to team process/effort, communications skills, groupthink, and effective use of conflict for creative and innovative ideas. Because all collaborative efforts are a unique mix of professionals, social structures, educational challenges, and community characteristics, each team should design its assessment activities to match its unique features, goals, and context.

FIGURE 6.4
Team Evaluation Exercise

1. *Task orientation* (integrity of problem-solving steps)

2. *Role clarification* (implicit and/or explicit agreement on and adherence to group roles, goals, and tasks relative to problem context)

3. *Communication/collaboration* (clear language; appropriate use of summarization; demonstration of trust and openness)

4. *Participation of group members* (shared responsibility in problem definition, problem analysis, plan development and plan evaluation; appropriate contributions relative to problem context)

5. *Conflict management* (problems identified and defined; differences in opinions and ideas clarified)

PROMISES AND PITFALLS

This chapter has confronted some of the features, challenges, costs, and rewards of collaboration among those possessing different professional specialties in schools. As with any worthwhile endeavor, collaborative multidisciplinary work groups include pitfalls and promises. An inappropriately strict adherence to collaborative work arrangements—when more effective and efficient means for achieving the work may exist—can result when enthusiasm for collaboration overrides the diagnosis of work needs, goals, and resources. Additionally, teams can suffer from groupthink or expend more energy making the group work than getting the job done. Finally, the social and technical features of the school, the work, and the goals to be achieved may be discounted in the team-structuring process, leading to a common organizational work dysfunction, displacement, as the structure becomes more important than the work.

The promises also are great. Interdependency and group autonomy bring to bear the combined resources of education professionals on students' problems, taking maximum advantage of the specialties that have developed to address the increasingly complex challenges of work in schools. Evidence exists that collaboration thus can better promote goal achievement and student success. Time demands and costs must be balanced, and the differences and needs of individual members taken into account, but great promise exists for the enhancement of school success.

REFERENCES

Angus, L. B. (1988, April). *School leadership and educational reform*. Paper presented at the annual meeting of the American Educational Research Association, New Orleans, Louisiana.

Bacharach, S. B., Bamberger, P., & Conley, S. (1990). Work process, role conflict, and role overload. *Journal of Work and Occupations, 17,* 199–228.

Bacharach, S. B., & Mundell, B. (1993). Organizational politics in schools: Micro, macro, and the logics of action. *Educational Administration Quarterly, 29,* 423–452.

Bauch, P. A., & Goldring, E. B. (1995). Parent involvement and school responsiveness: Facilitating the home-school connection in schools of choice. *Educational Evaluation and Policy Analysis, 17,* 1–21.

Bergan, J. R., & Dratochwill, T. R. (1990). *Behavioral consultation and therapy.* New York: Plenum.

Biddle, B. J. (1979). *Role theory: Expectations, identities, and behaviors.* New York: Plenum.

Bidwell, C., & Vreeland, R. S. (1977). Authority and control in client-serving organizations. In R. L. Blankenship (Ed.), *Colleagues in organization: The social construction of professional work* (pp. 360–370). New York: Wiley.

Brief, A. P., & Downey, H. K. (1983). Cognitive and organizational structures: A conceptual analysis of implicit organizing theories. *Human Relations, 36,* 1065–1090.

Brown, L. D. (1983). *Managing conflict at organizational interfaces.* Reading, MA: Addison-Wesley.

Capper, C. A. (1994)."We're not housed in an institution, we're housed in the community": Possibilities and consequences of neighborhood-based interagency collaboration. *Educational Administration Quarterly, 30,* 257–277.

Cherns, A. (1987). Principles of sociotechnical design revisited. *Human Relations, 40,* 153–162.

Chubb, J. E. (1988). Why the current wave of school reform will fail. *Public Interest, 90,* 28–49.

Chubb, J. E., & Moe T. M. (1988). *What price democracy? Politics, markets and American schools.* Washington, DC: Brookings Institution.

Chubb, J. E., & Moe, T. M. (1990). *Politics, markets, and America's schools.* Washington, DC: Brookings Institution.

Clark, C., Moss, P. A., Goering, S., Herter, R. J., Lamar, B., Leonard, D., Robbins, S., Russell, M., Templin, M., & Wascha, K. (1996). Collaboration as dialogue: Teachers and researchers engaged in conversation and professional development. *American Educational Research Journal, 33,* 193–231.

Conley, S. C., Bacharach, S. B., & Bauer, S. (1989). The school work environment and teacher career dissatisfaction. *Educational Administration Quarterly, 25,* 58–81.

Dean, J. W., Jr., & Brass, Daniel J. (1985). Social interaction and the perception of job characteristics in an organization. *Human Relations, 38,* 571–582,

DeLeon, P. H. (1995). Toward achieving multi disciplinary professional collaboration. *Professional Psychology, Research and Practice, 26,* 115–116.

Diamond, M. A., & Allcorn, S. (1985). Psychological dimensions of role use in bureaucratic organizations. *Organizational Dynamics, 14,* 35–59.

Duis, S. (1995, April). *Collaborative consultation: Are both school psychologists and teachers equally trained?* Paper presented at the annual meeting of the Council for Exceptional Children, Indianapolis, IN.

Friend, M., & Cook, L. (1990). Collaboration as a predictor for success in school reform. *Journal of Educational and Psychological Consultation, 1*, 69–86.

Gutkin, T. B., & Conoley, J. C. (1990). Reconceptualizing school psychology from a service delivery perspective: Implications for practice, training, and research. *Journal of School Psychology, 28*, 203–224.

Hart, A. W. (1987). Redesigning work for current and future teachers. In C. A. Bartell (Ed.), *Attracting excellence: Call for teacher incentives* (pp. 23–46). Elmhurst, IL: North Central Regional Educational Laboratory.

Hart, A. W. (1990a). Impacts of the school social unit on teacher authority during work redesign. *American Educational Research Journal, 27*, 503–532.

Hart, A. W. (1990b). Work redesign: A review of literature for education reform. In S. B. Bacharach (Ed.), *Advances in research and theories of school management* (Vol. 1, pp. 31–69). Greenwich, CT: JAI Press.

Hart, A. W. (1992, April). *Work feature values of tomorrow's teachers: Work redesign as an incentive and school improvement policy.* Paper presented at the annual meeting of the American Educational Research Association, San Francisco, CA.

Hart, A. W. (1994a). Creating teacher leadership roles: The impacts of core group support. *Educational Administration Quarterly, 30*, 472–497.

Hart, A. W. (1994b). Work feature values of today's and tomorrow's teachers: Work redesign as an incentive and school improvement policy. *Educational Evaluation and Policy Analysis, 16*(4), 458–473.

Hart, A. W. (1995). Reconceiving school leadership: Emergent views. *Elementary School Journal, 96*, 9–28.

Herman, S. M. (1994). *A force of ones: Reclaiming individual power in a time of teams, work groups, and other crowds.* San Francisco: Jossey-Bass.

Howard, H. A. (1994, November) Communication practices of yesteryear: A qualitative analysis of business and professional communication textbooks in the last ten years. Paper presented at the annual meeting of the Speech Communication Association, New Orleans, LA.

Janis, I. L. (1982). *Groupthink: Psychological studies of policy decisions and fiascoes.* Boston: Houghton Mifflin.

Johnson, D. W., & Johnson, F. P. (1987). *Joining together: Group therapy and group skills.* Englewood Cliffs, NJ: Prentice-Hall.

Johnson, L. J., Pugach, M., & Devlin, S. (1990). Professional collaboration. *Teaching Exceptional Children, 22*(2), 9–11.

Johnson, S. M. (1990a). Redesigning teachers' work. In R. F. Elmore, M. Cohen, J. L. David, H. D. Gideonse, S. M. Johnson, M. A. Raywid, B. Rowan, G. Sykes, *Restructuring schools: The next generation of educational reform.* San Francisco: Jossey-Bass.

Johnson, S. M. (1990b). *Teachers at work: Achieving success in our schools.* New York: Basic Books.

Jones, G. R. (1984). Task visibility, free riding, and shirking: Explaining the effect of structure and technology on employee behavior. *Academy of Management Review, 9*(4), 684–95.

Karge, B. D. (1995). The success of collaboration resource programs for students with disabilities in grades 6 though 8. *Remedial and Special Education, 16,* 79–89.

Keith, N. Z. (1996). A critical perspective on teacher participation in urban schools. *Educational Administration Quarterly, 32,* 45–79.

Kilgore, T. L., & Rubin, L. S. (1995). Collaboration for classroom behavior problems: Why it's difficult and how it can be implemented. *Teacher Education and Practice, 11,* 28–41.

Latack, J. C. (1984). Career transitions within organizations: An exploratory study of work, nonwork, and coping strategies. *Organizational Behavior and Human Performance, 34,* 296–322.

Lortie, D. C. (1975). *Schoolteacher: A sociological study.* Chicago, IL: University of Chicago Press.

Louis, M. R. (1980). Career transitions: Varieties and commonalities. *Academy of Management Review, 5*(3), 329–340.

Maeroff, G. I. (1993). *Team building for school change: Equipping teachers for new roles.* New York: Teachers College Press.

Malekoff, A., Johnson, H., & Klappersack, B. (1991, September). Parent-professional collaboration on behalf of children with learning disabilities. *Families in Society, 72,* 416–24.

Mayer, R. J. (1995). *Conflict management: The courage to confront* (2d ed.). Columbus, OH: Battelle Press.

Mitchell, S. M. (1986, April). *Negotiating the design of professional jobs.* Paper presented at the annual meeting of the American Educational Research Association, San Francisco.

Morris, J. (1992, September) Encouraging collaboration to keep kids in school and avoiding the duplication of effort. *Public Management, 74,* 3–7.

Muncey, D. E., & McQuillan, P. J. (1996). *Reform and resistance in schools and classrooms: An ethnographic view of the Coalition of Essential Schools.* New Haven, CT: Yale University Press.

Ogley, R. C. (1991). *Conflict under the microscope.* Bookfield, VT: Gower.

Pounder, D. G. (1995, October). *Faculty work teams: Paradoxical influences on teachers' work, work experiences and attitudes.* Paper presented at the annual meeting of the University Council for Educational Administration, Salt Lake City, UT.

Poole, W. (1995, April). *Reconstructing the teacher-administrator relationship to achieve systemic change.* Paper presented at the annual meeting of the American Educational Research Association, San Francisco, CA.

Schrage, M. (1990). *No more teams!* New York: Currency Doubleday.

Sheridan, S. M. (1990). Behavioral consultation with parents and teachers: Delivering treatment for socially withdrawn children at home and school. *School Psychology Review, 19,* 33– 52.

Siegel, J. A., & Colke, E. (1990). Role expansion for school psychologists: Challenges and future directions. In E. Coel & J. A. Siegel (Eds.), *Effective consultation in school psychology* (pp. 3–18). Toronto, Canada: Hogrefe & Huber.

Smylie, M. A. (1994). Redesigning teachers' work: Connections to the classroom. In L. Darling Hammond (Ed.), *Review of research in education* (Vol.

20, pp. 129–177). Washington, DC: American Educational Research Association.

Smylie, M. A., Lazarus, V., & Brownlee-Conyers, J. (1996). Instructional outcomes of school-based participative decision making. *Educational Evaluation and Policy Analysis, 18*(3), 181–198.

Stainbach, S., & Stainback, W. (1989). Integration of students with mild and moderate handicaps. In D. K. Lipsky & A. Gartner (Eds.), *Beyond separate education: Quality education for all* (pp. 41–52). Baltimore: Brookes.

Susskind, L., & Cruikshank, J. (1987). *Breaking the impasse: Consensual approaches to resolving public disputes.* New York: Basic Books.

Thomas, C. C., Correa, V. I., & Morsink, C. V. (1995). *Interactive teaming: Consultation and collaboration in special programs* (2d ed.). Englewood Cliffs, NJ: Prentice Hall.

Trist, E. L. (1981). *The evolution of sociotechnical systems.* Toronto: Ontario Quality of Working Life Centre.

Waller, W. (1932). *The sociology of teaching.* New York: Wiley.

Weeks, D. (1992). *The eight essential steps to conflict resolution: Preserving relationships at work, at home, and in the community.* Los Angeles: Tarcher.

Welch, M., & Sheridan, S. M. (1993). Educational partnerships in teacher education: Reconceptualizing how teacher candidates are prepared for teaching students with disabilities. *Action in Teacher Education, 15,* 35–46.

Welch, M., Sheridan, S. M., Fuhriman, A., Hart, A. W., Connell, M. L., & Stoddart, T. (1992). Preparing professionals for educational partnerships: An interdisciplinary approach. *Journal of Educational and Psychological Consultation, 3,* 1–23.

West, J. F. (1990). Educational collaboration in the restructuring of schools. *Journal of Educational and Psychological Consultation, 1,* 23–40.

White, J. A., & Wehlage, G. (1995). Community collaboration: If it is such a good idea, why is it so hard to do? *Educational Evaluation and Policy Analysis, 17,* 23–38.

Whyte, W. F. (1991). *Social theory for action: How individuals and organizations learn and change.* Newbury Park, CA: Sage.

Zins, J. E., Curits, M., Graden, J. L., & Ponti, C. R. (1988). *Helping children succeed in the regular classroom.* San Francisco: Jossey-Bass.

CHAPTER 7

Implications for Collaborative Instructional Practice

Karen Evans-Stout

A feeling of isolation describes that daunting moment when a new teacher, totally alone, first meets twenty to forty new faces and realizes the challenges ahead of her to make a positive difference in their lives. It also describes the emotions of that sleepless night before the first day of school, repeated again and again, year after year in a lifelong teaching career, meeting new faces and continually starting over, hoping to avoid the mistakes made last year—and, as on that first day of teaching, facing all these moments essentially alone. Isolated, of course, describes more than an emotion. It also describes traditional teaching practice—closing the classroom door and then learning by trial and error through one's own mistakes, experimenting with new approaches in private, solving problems of practice through one's own initiative and creativity, and meeting the needs of students—alone.

Although the culture of schools, and teaching especially, has been largely a culture of privacy and isolation, that does not necessarily imply effects all to the negative. On the contrary, the teacher who succeeds under isolated conditions develops a powerful sense of autonomy and independence and can claim to have made it "on her own." The special relationships that develop between a teacher and her students in a largely isolated classroom also provide a unique intrinsic reward for the teacher. Being able to claim personal responsibility for success is so much a part of American individualism that it probably helps to explain why this culture continues to dominate instructional practice.

Many authors argue, however, that the culture of isolation, with its claims to privacy and individualism, is one of the greatest hindrances to improved practice and to the inferred consequent of improved practice—improved student achievement (Louis, Kruse, & Bryk, 1995; Little, 1982; Lortie, 1975; Rosenholtz, 1985). They maintain that a teacher alone should no longer bear the sole responsibility for a student's success for one entire school year at the elementary level. Nor should one teacher in a secondary school take full responsibility in a subject area. Everyone in a school is responsible for student learning. No longer should a special education teacher pull out students for remediation and work with them alone in a tiny office. No longer should a principal or department head make curriculum decisions without input from others. No longer must a principal bear all the responsibility for difficult disciplinary actions. Instead, professionals in education, as in other occupations, can share tasks and responsibilities through the process of collaboration, collaboration that goes beyond simple collegiality—"mutual learning and discussion of classroom practice and student performance" (Louis et al., 1995, p. 33)—to an interdependency that leads to shared responsibility and shared understandings, which may transform the educators involved, their instructional practices, and the context in which they work.

There are any number of collaborative arrangements presently in use in schools. Site-based teams with managerial decision-making powers, curriculum teams, grade-level or department teams, interdisciplinary teams, and teams formed in response to particular problems are just some examples of the collaboration in schools. Additionally, there are many new players on the teams, including parents, community resource people, and special educators. Clearly, the opportunities to collaborate have broadened.

The focus of this chapter is collaboration around teaching or instruction, for that is the fundamental focus of practice in schools. Collaborative arrangements that have primary responsibility for teaching and learning can take many forms, including a team composed of two friends who come together as partners, the team formed by a mentor and a person seeking guidance, a teacher team with a teacher leader, an interdisciplinary team with members from core subject areas, a team that includes special educators, a department team, or some combination of such teams. Because much of the available literature outside of special education focuses on teacher teams in middle schools—either interdisciplinary or departmentalized—and also similar teaming arrangements in elementary and high schools, this discussion primarily draws from research on those teacher teaming arrangements.

I begin by discussing some of the background and roots of instructional collaboration—because, like most "new" ideas in education, collaboration has a history. Next I consider some of the promises and pitfalls of collaboration for instructional improvement. Then I discuss the changing context of education and some of the tensions of classroom practice that have implications for instructional collaboration. Finally, I offer some recomendations for those considering collaboration as a means for instructional innovation and improvement.

BACKGROUND

Team teaching as it is currently practiced was conceived in the 1950s as a way to efficiently utilize staff for the improvement of scientific and technological education (Armstrong, 1977). The innovation is credited to Francis Keppel and Judson T. Shaplin, both associated with the Harvard Graduate School of Education (Blair and Woodard, 1964, as quoted in Barnett, 1982). Early implementations stressed efficient use of staff as the main strength of teacher teaming, since there was a shortage of staff at that time to meet the demands placed on schools following the launching of Sputnik (Barnett, 1982).

It was not long after the formal articulation of team teaching that other researchers postulated advantages for it (see, e.g., Chamberlin, 1969; Giltman, 1965; Lobb; 1965; White, 1964). Goodlad and Anderson (1969) noted that teaming allowed flexibility in grouping of students. The close communication afforded teachers allowed them to quickly adjust plans by analyzing, prescribing, and carrying out plans repeatedly. These authors felt that working cooperatively forced teachers to consider all factors in making decisions; these factors included the subject matter, interests of the learners, student differences, teacher strengths and weakness, and resources.

In a 1977 review of team teaching, Armstrong compiled the claims for team teaching into a list of five strengths:

1. Effective utilization of teacher strengths in planning and delivering instruction
2. Motivation for creativity because teachers have an audience of peers and students
3. Facilitation of individualized instruction
4. Better sequencing and pacing of instruction
5. The building of program continuity

Although many authors spoke to the assumed strengths of team teaching, Armstrong (1977) noted the paucity of empirical studies about achievement with teaming, especially in light of the early support for the concept. He concluded that most of the studies reviewed found no significant differences in achievement between team-taught students and those taught by one teacher alone at the elementary or high school levels. He also identified several problems in the research that have been noted in other reviews since (Arhar, Johnston, & Markle, 1989; Cotton, 1982; St. Clair & Hough, 1992). These include inconsistent attention to the integrity of the intervention, short duration of the studies with longitudinal data nonexistent, and poor designs that failed to eliminate confounding variables that affect student achievement (e.g., other innovations in use such as flexible scheduling, use of tutors). Clearly the database from the 1960s and 1970s is limited and indicates that our knowledge of the effects of teaming on student achievement is sadly wanting.

For the most part, more recent discussions about collaboration have focused on the organizational conditions that support joint work, rather than the consequences of that work. Cousins, Ross, and Maynes (1994) argue that the benefits of instructional collaboration can largely be characterized as improved teacher work life—including enhanced social relations with other teachers, sense of belonging, work enjoyment, change of pace, relief from job-related stress, a more well-rounded picture of students and, thereby, the sense of being more effective with students. However, the leap to improved student achievement is more difficult to confirm. The argument, according to these authors, is as follows: organizational conditions lead to joint work, which in turn supports the implementation of improved instructional practice, which leads to improved student achievement. But they believe that a black box lies between instructional implementation and student outcomes. We still do not have much evidence suggesting which collaborative instructional practices lead to improved student learning.

PROMISES AND PITFALLS FOR INSTRUCTIONAL IMPROVEMENT

The early team teaching literature may be limited in its details about student achievement effects; nevertheless, team teaching has persisted as a promising organizational arrangement for the renewal of schools. Today, however, the arguments that promote it are even more ambitious. Proponents argue that the potential to influence instructional improvement exists when collaborative arrangements expand student, teacher, and organizational capacities. Little (1990, p. 523) explains, "teachers, as members of an 'occupational community' exert reciprocal influence on one another and on the school as an organization in the interests of a student clientele for whom they accept joint responsibility . . . each one's success is everyone's responsibility." She further argues that for teachers to profit from teaming, its advantages must be linked closely to the task of teaching. She believes that the motivation for collaboration centers on the work of teaching, because it is through teaching that teachers derive professional satisfaction. She notes collaborative instructional arrangements can influence: (1) students' opportunity to learn, (2) teachers' improved image and capacity in technical aspects of practice, and (3) school improvement from collective decision making on curriculum, instruction, and testing (see also Pounder, chap. 5, this text).

Specifically, teacher teaming allows for better use of resources (Little, 1990). It may be textbooks, original source materials that can be scarce in classrooms, facilities, or time, but sharing can make resources go further and reach more students. The greatest resource that becomes shared is teacher expertise (see also Pounder, chap. 5, this text). Interdisciplinary teaming assumes that teachers will share their areas of expertise with the team. For example, one person may have exceptional content knowledge about a particular area, and that person now becomes accessible to all students for whom the team shares responsibility. Some teachers are particularly effective teaching one-on-one, while others are stronger in large groups. Some teachers orchestrate cooperative groups well. Now all these various strengths can be effectively utilized by the team.

As resources are shared, the act of teaching becomes more visible, resulting in a host of effects. Visibility can promote creativity as one now teaches for a larger audience, including one's peers. Evaluations by colleagues are more significant than evaluation by the principal (Johnston, Markle, & Arhar, 1988) and act as a powerful motivator. Motivated to do well in front of others, one becomes willing to learn—especially in an atmosphere of trust. Rosenholtz (1989) found that teachers in isolated settings reported that their professional learning was limited to the first two years of practice, while teachers in collaborative arrangements believed that teaching is complex and involves continuous learning. Additionally, as a teacher teaches, he or she communicates beliefs about both teaching and learning. These now become public and, in an atmosphere of trust and learning, open to examination.

Visibility of one's practice and the sharing that can follow communicate beliefs about pupils and expectations for them (Little, 1990). Instructional priorities are revealed and open to scrutiny. A problem with a student in a traditional teacher-led classroom is a one-on-one problem. Now such problems can be shared and a variety of solutions accessed. Johnston et al. (1988) note that teaming results in more asking for help with difficult students, and the development of group-efficacy for solving complex problems of practice.

Although the effects on instructional practice are still inadequately documented, one positive benefit is that teaming promotes collegial decisions about instruction (Johnston et al., 1988; Little, 1990). If a task is complex and responsibility is shared, there is more teacher interdependence, as teachers are more likely to ask for help (Johnston et al., 1988; Little, 1990). There is also more willingness to take risks if one does not have to stand alone; it is safer to try an innovation as a team (Johnston et al., 1988).

When the culture of isolation is challenged by collaboration and shared responsibility, many benefits such as those described above are possible. However, instructional collaboration also has its potential pitfalls. Much of the research on teaming suggests that the maximum benefits are not always realized. It is evident that the teacher gives up the ability to take individual action. Although she may have an individual preference, she looses the latitude to act and the privacy to do so without scrutiny; instead, she is held accountable to the team (Little, 1990) and must uphold team decisions. But, according to Little (1990), just as the teacher becomes more publicly scrutinized, she also receives collective support for her teaching skills, her content and pedagogical knowledge, and her decision making ability.

In a set of case studies from the Coalition of Essential Schools (Muncey & McQuillan, 1996), one frustration that teachers noted was loosing their sense of the flow of instruction. An experienced teacher has an intuitive sense of whether students understand what is being taught, what they need to learn next, and how to handle the difficulties that arise. In a shared situation, that intuition may be undermined. As one teacher put it:

> I was a successful teacher . . . I knew where all the signposts were so that if something was going badly, I could see the signposts and I could improve it. And if something was going well, I could foster that . . . Suddenly (after being put on a team), everything that I knew I could do was cut down to a few things I was supposed to do, and I didn't have any of those signposts that would reinforce that I was doing a good job. (Muncey & McQuillan, 1996, pp. 169–170)

Teachers with a history of successful practice may find their intuitive craft knowledge irrelevant in a setting in which the control of instruction is shared. Inevitably, teachers may sacrifice some intrinsic rewards such as pride in students who succeed under their tutelage or the enjoyment of autonomously running their own classrooms (Cousins, Ross, & Maynes, 1994).

Teaming among colleagues who do not share similar perspectives on how to best meet student needs lead to significant tension. To function effectively, the team must negotiate differences in values by establishing priorities (Cousins et al., 1994). Because one does not always work with like-minded colleagues, conflict is part of the work in teams (Little, 1990), and that conflict can be the reason for one of the findings in the early teaming literature—that teams often avoid conflict and make only low-level decisions—a finding that persists in the current literature. For example, in a study about a teacher team in a primary school that was appointed to set a schoolwide behavior management policy, Johnston and Hedemann (1994) found that "Discussions among the committee members stayed largely on safe topics associated with school rules and discipline in the playground" (p. 306). In another study of team discussions in a middle school, Blomquist et al. (1986) found that weekly meetings tended to focus on discussing individual students and that there was little sharing about ideas and materials (see also Pounder, chap. 5, this text). Little (1990) also notes that to avoid conflict teacher teams may make only easy decisions—decisions that "have only marginal significance for the lives of either students or teachers" (p. 522).

In a study that looked at collegial interactions, Zahorik (1987) found that although teachers helped each other with problems about materials, discipline, classroom learning activities, and learning problems of individual students, more complex problems of practice such as implementing specific pedagogies, achieving goals and objectives, and student evaluation were less frequent. The teachers in this study argued that they talk less about these things because the associated behaviors are more personal, private, and intuitive (as discussed in Rowan, 1990). Zahorik concluded that the "shallow" (p. 394) nature of the discussions does not support deep change in teaching practices.

The nature of teacher talk in teams is not always professionally oriented. In order to avoid conflict teachers may focus on the superficial and ignore the larger philosophical questions that influence teaching behaviors. The result may be to perpetuate entrenched practices. Teaming becomes focused largely on splitting up tasks, discussing individual students, and sharing physical resources rather than on influencing the thinking of others or their classroom performance (Little, 1990). As Arhar et al. state: "A single organizational arrangement does not assure that collaboration will occur on such important matters as instructional improvement or curricular integration" (1988, p. 25).

In sum, collaboration promises to mitigate the effects of the culture of isolation and privacy that has characterized American teaching practice. Collaborative organizational arrangements encourage interdependency when teachers: (1) share the responsibility and rewards for the success of a shared group of students, (2) can learn from each other in an atmosphere of safety in displaying one's practice, (3) can discuss practical and philosophical issues of practice, and (4) can experiment with innovative teaching methods to improve student achievement. The pitfalls of collaboration occur over the loss of the intrinsic rewards of complex student/teacher relationships and over conflict around intuitive and deeply held beliefs about teaching craft and student learning.

CURRENT CONTEXTUAL CONSIDERATIONS

During the last fifteen years education has experienced reforms that continue to exert a variety of influences. The current wave of reform, restructuring (Passow, 1990), like other reform efforts, takes as its foremost goal academic improvement for all students (Cohen, 1990; Elmore, 1990; Fuhrman, 1993). Today, however, academic improvement means more than teaching for coverage and the learning of basic skills and facts. Instead, the emphasis is on teaching for in-depth understanding and learning in a rich, authentic context such that opportunities for transfer are enhanced (Cognition and Technology Group at Vanderbilt, 1990; Cole, 1990). The belief that such a level of learning is possible in all students rests on the view that learning is knowledge construction (Derry, 1992), and concomitant with that view have been a host of new curricular and instructional developments.

Derry notes that the metaphor of learning as knowledge construction has spawned a host of related metaphors for schools and learning. She cites: "learning as enculturation, problem solving as knowledge negotiation, schools as communities of practice, instructional activities as communities of practice, learning as apprenticeship" (p. 417). Central to these metaphors is a view of school learning as authentic, whole to part, and developmentally oriented with activities that support a recursive construction of knowledge. Knowledge is "situated" in culture (Brown, Collins, & Duguid, 1989) and embedded in activity rather than removed from context.

Such a view of teaching and learning is child centered as opposed to teacher centered, an arrangement in which the teacher stands in the front and "delivers" the lesson using such methods as direct instruction or effective instructional techniques. The student assumes more responsibility for learning, but the teacher, rather than delivering a lesson, has more responsibility for fostering conditions for learning. This means developing activities in which knowledge or content is embedded, not explicitly taught. It means being able to accept a range of unintended outcomes as students essentially form their own constructions based on their prior learnings and present constructions. What has emerged as instructional models are the whole language approach, learning math through manipulatives, a problem solving approach to science, and process writing (Lieberman, 1994). All of these methods assume classroom practice centered around disciplined inquiry, trust, openness, and collaboration (Lieberman, 1994).

At odds with this current instructional reform emphasis is the strong pattern of stability (or arguably inertia) regarding instructional practice in schools. The history of instructional change throughout several reforms is not encouraging—instructional practice has stayed largely the same (Cohen, 1988; Cuban, 1984, 1986; Marshall, 1992). In *A Place Called School* (1984), Goodlad noted that in the thousand schools participating in the study, instruction largely consisted of lecturing, explaining, and monitoring seatwork. Cuban has written extensively about the "durability of teacher-centered instruction." Tye (1987) refers to a "deep structure of schooling" that includes the underlying maintenance of control evident in pedagogy, programs, and policies (see also Barott & Raybould, chap. 2, this text).

Related to the tension between newer student-centered approaches to instruction and long-established traditional instructional approaches is the "tension between individual and social standards [that] seems to be at the very heart of teachers' work" (Lampert, 1984, p. 11). Lampert (1985) argues that teaching is conflict "management," living with ambiguity, realizing that there are no clear right or wrong solutions to many of the decisions that must be made. One continual source of conflict is the tension between the needs of students and the standards of the institution (Lampert, 1984). Students bring a unique set of experiences to school learning and interpret in unique ways what they are taught. At the same time the school and society define what *all* students should know and be able to do. The teacher is continually negotiating a contradiction between novel, customized, and often trial-and-error approaches to individual student learning versus institutional demands for uniformity, standardization, and "right" answers.

Perhaps it would be easier for teachers to close their classroom doors and balance these continual contradictions in private rather than to openly negotiate these tensions with a group of peer teachers. This may explain, in part, the strong norm of privacy and independence that characterizes teaching (Little, 1990). It follows that the limited peer input from others about a teacher's craft contributes to the "sameness" of instructional practice in spite of reform efforts.

To what degree are collaborative teaching arrangements likely to facilitate newer student-centered learning as knowledge construction instructional approaches? Instructional collaboration would require teachers to openly negotiate the contradictions described above to arrive at some common instructional action. The act of resolving instructional contradictions would involve establishing priorities (Lampert, 1984) around competing values. Unfortunately, collaborative teaching groups often focus largely on shallow discussions around grouping, scheduling, and dividing tasks (Little, 1990) rather than engaging in substantive discussions about philosophical and value differences. Having been enculturated into a norm of respect for individuality, autonomy, and noninterference, and without the experience of negotiating differences, teachers may ignore the larger questions about practice in spite of the opportunity created by group collaboration.

These powerful contextual tensions may influence whether teaming can succeed as a means to support new views of instruction. Teaching has been resistant to change over many reforms, and this may well be because the negotiating that teachers must do between managing the process of student learning and responding to public accountability standards is easier to do with the classroom door closed, in private, without trying to negotiate priorities with a team of teachers who hold differing values. Although teacher teams hold the potential for challenging conventional approaches to teaching, they are unlikely to realize this potential unless they become more comfortable openly addressing conflict and competing priorities.

RECOMMENDATIONS

The above discussion of the history, promises and pitfalls, and contextual considerations of instructional collaboration lead me to several recommendations. I believe that at least four conditions must be met for improved instructional practice to occur as a result of collaborative instructional arrangements. First, collaboration takes time (Muncey & McQuillan, 1996). It requires time for team relationships to develop so that teachers understand each other's educational orientations and styles. It requires time to observe and learn about the strengths and weaknesses each brings to the team, and learning from others through observation of their practice and consultation is a slow process. Nowacek (1992) notes that "the knowledge exchange seem(s) to occur by osmosis rather than by injection" (p. 276). In a study about a school founded to utilize shared decision making and teacher teams, Lonnquist and King (1993) noted that the lack of time given for the teams to develop was critical in the failure of the school. As one teacher commented: "I think if any school wants to do this kind of model where we really try to create a team of teachers, you need to have that team have a chance to create itself" (p. 12).

For collaboration to succeed, the second condition is trust (see also

Galvin, chap. 4, this text). Sometimes teachers avoid discussions about values because they are hard to resolve (Little, 1990). However, what is necessary may not be resolution but, rather, trust that there is more than one way to serve students. Thus teachers can continue to value their individual views about how to best serve students while building an atmosphere of acceptance and respect for multiple perspectives. This trust allows the "thoughtful, explicit examination of practices and their consequences" (Little, 1990) so that a norm of open professional work discussions supplants the existing privacy norm.

The third condition required for collaboration is tenacity—change takes persistence. Too often in education we abandon a good idea before it has time to realize its full potential. We must be committed to the long haul—to stay the course—to "hang in there" if we expect change to occur. Adults prefer stability in their lives (Atchley, 1989), so they resist change that is uncertain. They need patience to experience the success and benefits of new practices and new norms of practice.

Finally, for collaboration to enhance instructional practice, the patterns of interactions among teachers must transform from shallow conversations to deep discussions on practice, values, instructional methods, and conceptions of learning. Shared responsibility for student success and teacher success can foster interdependency rather than teams that practice as individuals working side-by-side. As instructional practice "matures," teachers may find themselves able to be both autonomous and interdependent—or individually different while mutually dependent.

CONCLUSION

Several arguments undergird the emphasis on instructional collaboration rather than the privacy that has traditionally characterized instructional practice. Most of these arguments concern improved teacher work lives, assuming a link between improved instructional practice and student learning that is largely unsubstantiated. If educators are to sustain this innovation, then research is sorely needed to verify that collaboration favorably affects instructional practice and student achievement. More specifically, research must examine teacher productivity and student opportunity to learn. It must consider what influences teachers have on each other's instructional practices. Does the work teachers do in teams differ signficantly from work done in isolation, and how does it differ? Research must also consider what conditions of collaboration affect instructional practice, and what practices lead to improved achievement. Are there any ways in which teaming maximizes newer models of instruction? What are they?

It makes intuitive sense that breaking down the isolation that has pervaded teaching practice would improve teacher work life, teacher learning, and teacher practice. It also seems to follow that improving these things would affect student achievement—but that inference is more tenuous. Without evidence of that link, the future of teacher teaming is uncertain. Strong norms of privacy may prevail as teachers attempt to balance individual student needs and institutional goals. When the rewards of teaching largely reside in the complex relationships developed with students in the privacy of the classroom, teachers will need convincing evidence that collaborating with others can lead to improved ways to meet student needs. It is only by answering the deeper questions about the link between collaborative practice and improved student outcomes that teacher teaming can survive.

REFERENCES

Arhar, J. M., Johnston, J. H., & Markle, G. C. (1988). The effects of teaming on students. *Middle School Journal, 19*(5), 22–25.

Armstrong, D. G. (1977). Team teaching and academic achievement. *Review of Educational Research, 47*(1), 65–86.

Atchley, R. (1989). A continuity theory of normal aging. *The Gerontologist, 29*, 183–190.

Barnett, C. W. (1982). *Team teaching in the elementary school.* Palo Alto, CA: R & E Research Associates.

Blair, M. & Woodard, R. G. (1964). *Team teaching in action.* Boston: Houghton Mifflin.

Blomquist, R., Bornstein, S., Fink, G., Michaud, R., Oja, S. N., & Smulyan, L. (1986). *Action research on change in schools: The relationship between teacher moral/job satisfaction and organizational changes in a junior high school* (Report no. 81–0040). Washington DC: National Institute of Education.

Brown, J. S., Collins, A., & Duguid. (1989). Situated cognition and the culture of learning. *Educational Researcher, 18*(1), 32–42.

Chamberlin, L. J. (1969). *Team teaching: Organization and administration.* Columbus, OH: Merrill.

Cognition and Technology Group at Vanderbilt (1990). Anchored instruction and its relationship to situated cognition. *Educational Researcher, 19*(6), 1–10.

Cohen, D. K. (1988). *Teaching practice: Plus ca change. . . .* East Lansing: Michigan State University, National Center Research on Teacher Education.

Cohen, M. (1990). Key issues confronting state policymakers. In R. Elmore (Ed.), *Restructuring schools: The next generation of educational reform* (pp. 251–288). San Francisco: Jossey Bass.

Cole, N. S. (1990). Conceptions of educational achievement. *Educational Researcher, 19*(3), 2–7.

Cotton, K. (1982). Effects of interdisciplinary team teaching. Portland, OR: Northwest Regional Education Lab (ERIC Documentation Reproduction Service No. ED 230 533).

Cousins, J. B., Ross, J. A., & Maynes, F. J. (1994). The reported nature and consequences of teachers' joint work in three exemplary schools. *The Elementary School Journal, 94*, 441–465.

Cuban, L. (1984). *How teachers taught*. New York: Longman.

Cuban, L. (1986). Persistant instruction: Another look at constancy in the classroom. *Phi Delta Kappan, 68*, 7–11.

Derry, S. J. (1992). Beyond symbolic process: Expanding horizons for educational psychology. *Journal of Educational Psychology, 84*(4), 413–418.

Elmore, R. F. (1990). Introduction: On changing the structure of public schools. In R. Elmore (Ed.), *Restructuring schools: The next generation of educational reform* (pp. 1–28). San Francisco: Jossey Bass.

Fuhrman, S. H. (1993). The politics of coherence. In S. H. Fuhrman (Ed.), *Designing coherent educational policy: Improving the system* (pp. 1–34). San Francisco: Jossey Bass.

Giltinan, B. (1965). The rise and demise of a team. *English Journal, 54*, 429–432.

Goodlad, J. I. (1984). *A place called school: Prospects for the future*. New York: McGraw Hill.

Goodlad, J. I., & Anderson, R. (1969). *The nongraded elementary school*. New York: Harcourt, Brace, and World.

Johnston, J. H., Markle, G. C., & Arhar, J. M. (1988). Cooperation, collaboration, and the professional development of teachers. *Middle School Journal, 19*(4), 28–32.

Johnston, S. & Hedemann, M. (1994). School level curriculum decisions—a case of battling against the odds. *Educational Review, 46*(3), 297–308.

Lampert, M. (1984). Teaching about thinking and thinking about teaching. *Journal of Curriculum Studies, 16*(1), 1–18.

Lampert, M. (1985). How do teacher manage to teach? Perspectives on problems in practice. *Harvard Educational Review, 55*(2), 178–194.

Lieberman, A. (1994). Teacher development: Commitment and challenge. In P. P. Grimmett and J. Neufeld (Eds.), *Teacher development and the struggle for authenticity* (pp. 15–29). New York: Teachers College Press.

Little, J. W. (1982). Norms of collegiality and experimentation: Workplace conditions of school success. *American Educational Research Journal, 19*, 325–340.

Little, J. W. (1990). The persistence of privacy: Autonomy and initiative in teachers' professional relations. *Teachers College Record, 91*(4), 509–536.

Lobb, M. D. (1965). *Practical aspects of team teaching*. Dubuque, IA: William C. Brown.

Lonnquist, M. P., & King, J. A. (1993). *Changing the tire on a moving bus: Barriers to the development of professional community in a new teacher-led school*. Minneapolis: University of Minnesota, Center for Applied Research and Educational Improvement.

Lortie, D. C. (1975). *Schoolteacher: A sociological study*. Chicago, IL: University of Chicago Press.

Louis, K. S., Kruse, S. D., & Bryk, A. S. (1995). Professionalism and community: What is it and why is it important in urban schools? In K. S. Louis and S. D. Kruse (Eds.), *Professionalism and community: Perspectives on reforming urban schools* (pp. 3–22). Thousand Oaks, CA: Corwin Press.

Marshall, H. H. (1992). Seeing, redefining, and supporting student learning. In H. H. Marshall (Ed.), *Redefining learning: Roots of educational change* (pp. 1–32). Norwood, NJ: Ablex.

Muncey, D. E., & McQuillan, P. J. (1996). *Reform and resistance in schools and classrooms: An ethnographic view of the Coalition of Essential Schools.* New Haven, CT: Yale University Press.

Nowacek, E. J. (1992). Professionals talk about teaching together: Interviews with five collaborating teachers. *Intervention in School and Clinic, 27*(5), 262–276.

Passow, A. H. (1990). How it happened, wave by wave. In B. S. Bacharach (Ed.), *Educational reform: Making sense of it all* (pp. 10–19). Boston: Allyn & Bacon.

Rowan, B. (1990). Commitment and control: Alternative strategies for the organizational design of schools. *Review of Research in Education, 16,* 353–389.

Rosenholtz, S. (1985). Political myths about education reform: Lessons from research on teaching. *Phi Delta Kappan, 66,* 349–355.

Rosenholtz, S. (1989). *Teachers' workplace.* New York: Longman.

St. Clair, B., & Hough, D. L. (1992). Interdisciplinary teaching: A review of the literature. Southwest Missouri State University: Dept. of Curriculum & Instruction. (ERIC Document Reproduction Service No. ED 373 056.)

Tye, B. B. (1987). The deep structure of schooling. *Phi Delta Kappan, 69,* 281–284.

White, R. W. (1964). How successful is team teaching? *Science Teacher, 31*(6), 34–37.

Zahorik, J. A. (1987). Teachers' collegial interaction: An exploratory study. *Elementary School Journal, 87,* 385–396.

CHAPTER 8

Implications for Leadership
in Collaborative Schools

Gary M. Crow

Few conceptual or empirical examinations of leadership in collaborative schools exist beyond normative views of what should be. This makes it difficult to know how to talk about leadership in a way that makes sense within the current realities of schools. For example, inherent in calls for collaboration is an expansion of leadership roles. Regardless of whether we are describing internal school collaboration or interagency collaboration, we typically assume that leadership is shared and dispersed throughout the school and its environment. According to the normative view, collaboration should expand the quantity of school leadership, that is, more people should become leaders. This raises issues of definition and agency: What constitutes leadership and who are the leaders and followers?

Also according to a normative perspective, collaboration should expand the spheres of leadership. Proponents of interagency collaboration, for example, assume that leadership exists throughout the school environment, both internally and externally. This obviously raises issues of control and coordination for school administrators: Who is responsible and accountable for various actions?

These issues and assumptions raise questions about how to understand and talk about leadership in collaborative settings and the implications of this for school administrators. This chapter attempts to clarify some of our understanding about leadership in collaborative school settings, beginning with a conception of leadership based on the two issues raised above: the quantity and spheres of leadership. Following this, the chapter reviews literature on leadership in reform settings. Finally, the chapter discusses implications for school administrators that include the promises and pitfalls of leadership in collaborative school settings.

A CONCEPTION OF LEADERSHIP FOR COLLABORATION

Leadership in collaborative settings includes two primary features: leadership as an influence relationship and leadership as systemic. The first involves a political act, while the second involves the institutional environment in which schools exist in collaborative relationships. These two features emphasize the uniqueness of leadership in collaborative settings and influence the promises and pitfalls of leadership for collaboration.

Leadership as an Influence Relationship

Historically leadership has been examined and understood in a variety of ways. One categorization suggests six major themes: "leadership as a personal quality, a type of behavior, dependent on the situation, a relationship, an organizational feature, and a moral quality" (Crow, Matthews, & McLeary, 1996, p. 9). The first three of these themes characterize leadership as leaders—their traits, their behaviors and their response to different situations. Equating leadership with leaders has been criticized for its narrowness, but it retains its potency in our common language about leadership. When reform literature in education describes principals as instructional leaders, this view is implicit.

Yukl (1994) identifies a major controversy surrounding the understanding of leadership as the debate between those who see leadership as an individual quality and those who see it as an organizational one. Recent restructuring reforms, such as collaboration, argue for a conception of leadership that de-emphasizes the agency of a single individual and stresses the relationship between leaders and followers, thus putting the focus on leadership rather than leaders. Instead of examining what leaders are and do, we look at what leadership means within the relationship among leaders and followers.

Understanding leadership as a relationship involves looking beyond formal authority as the source of leadership. Leaders may be formal authorities but may just as likely be those without formal authority. Rost (1991) argues that while authority may be necessary for a managerial relationship it is not necessary for a leadership relationship. Formal authority is not the sole basis of leadership in part because, as we will discuss later, leadership relationships are based on additional resources other than authority, for example, expertise and interpersonal skills.

Leadership as a relationship involves the active participation of both leaders and followers. Instead of putting the usual emphasis on what leaders do, this view recognizes and values the active role of followers. Kelley (1992) suggests three ways exemplary followers contribute to their organizations: they prove their value to the organization, build webs of relationships, and exhibit a courageous conscience. Instead of being seen as taking a passive role (the one assigned to followers when the emphasis is on leadership as an individual quality), followers are perceived as necessary for leadership to occur.

This conception of leadership is characterized by a particular type of relationship between leaders and followers. The leadership relationship involves influence: both leaders and followers actively attempt to influence each other toward some purpose. Rost (1991) defines leadership as "an influence relationship among leaders and followers who intend real change that reflects their mutual purposes" (p. 102). By defining leadership in this way, Rost can highlight the active pursuit of both leaders and followers to influence each other in pursuit of some larger purpose. He argues that this is what Burns (1978) intends by "transformational leadership."

Teachers and principals may be in an influence relationship where both are leaders and followers at different times. Teachers, for example, lead by influencing other teachers to adopt particular visions of the school or school improvement strategies. They also influence the principal by urging acceptance of new curriculum reforms. Yet teachers are also active followers in an influence relationship with principals. Their particular areas of expertise and the types of relationships they have developed with each other or with parents may influence the principal to initiate particular school reforms or to take on particular leadership styles that fit with a collective vision of the school. They also may subtly influence by halfheartedly responding to principal leadership behavior they find unpersuasive or unpleasant, for example, dictatorial styles, in an attempt to get the principal to adopt more democratic styles and behavior.

Principals can also be active leaders and followers. As leaders, principals can attempt to persuade teachers to accept and support a particular vision of the school. They may also act in a leadership capacity by supporting and developing the leadership potential of teachers. But they also may be active followers, responding to the leadership of teachers. For example, encouraging teachers' visions of the school and championing the change strategies being promoted by teacher leaders are significant acts of followership.

These illustrations of the influence relationship among teachers and principals demonstrate how leadership is dynamic in determining who are leaders and followers. Instead of taking a normative view that claims all teachers should be leaders, we can better understand leadership in dynamic terms in which the characterization of leader and follower change at different times for different purposes (Firestone, 1996; Hart, 1995).

Leaders and followers in an influence relationship use various "power resources to persuade others" (Rost, 1991). In its early stages, the literature on leadership as a relationship was one sided, focusing on the influence tactics of leaders. However, more recent research has identified the influence tactics used by followers. For example, Blase (1989) identifies the tactics used by teachers to influence principals, for example, diplomacy, conformity, extra work, visibility, avoidance, ingratiation, and threats. Rost (1991) argues that both leaders and followers use power resources to influence each other, for example, expertise, position, reasoned argument, reputation, prestige, personality, purpose, status, content of the message, and interpersonal and group skills. We should not assume that these power resources are evenly distributed: leaders and followers both use power resources to influence each other.

Collaboration and Leadership as an Influence Relationship

Leadership as an influence relationship makes sense in collaborative settings. Collaboration is sometimes depicted as if individuals easily reach a consensus by simple rational discussion. Such a view is seldom realistic. Although collaboration may involve peaceful cooperation, it is just as likely to involve intense attempts to persuade others regarding the best way to change schools. Persuasion may use reasoned argument, but it may just as well involve the use of power resources such as expertise, reputation, interpersonal skills, and status. To assume an unrealistic and apolitical view of leadership for collaboration is to misinterpret the nature of collaboration.

Two major features of collaboration are critical to our understanding of leadership: *parity* and *reciprocity* (Mergondoller, 1981). Parity involves establishing equal status among participants. In order for collaboration to occur, all parties must have some power resources at their disposal. If one side can coerce the other because it alone possesses resources, neither collaboration nor leadership occurs. Leadership for collaboration involves an influence relationship where parity is possible.

The second feature of collaboration is reciprocity. Collaboration involves an active exchange in which both leaders and followers believe they are receiving privileges, benefits, and rewards for the effort they have provided. Such an exchange is necessary for collaboration, because parties must believe they are meeting their needs and accomplishing their mutual purposes (Burns, 1978)

Both parity and reciprocity are inherent in collaboration and make leadership in these settings a political relationship. In the influence relationship within a collaborative setting, both leaders and followers are attempting to establish parity and reciprocity. By using power resources, these individuals seek to establish and maintain their status and enter an exchange relationship to optimize each other's rewards and further their mutual purposes.

Leadership as Systemic

Previous chapters in this book have delineated the expanding spheres in which collaboration exists and thus present the need to develop a conception of leadership that allows for this. Collaboration occurs both inside the school and outside the school with other organizations. Leadership in such a setting must acknowledge this expansive quality.

For purposes of understanding leadership in a collaborative setting, we will use and expand on the literature that treats leadership as systemic. Ogawa and Bossert, in a 1995 article on leadership as an organizational quality, refer to the conceptual roots of this position (Barnard, 1968; Cartwright, 1965; Katz & Kahn, 1966; Tannenbaum, 1962; Thompson, 1967). These roots move us beyond thinking of leadership as an individual attribute to a quality that "varies across organizations and even within organizations over time" (Ogawa & Bossert, 1995, p. 226).

Ogawa and Bossert argue that leadership as an organizational quality involves an influence relationship but that it moves beyond the simple influence of individuals to the influence of the system. Using institutional theory, they emphasize leadership as influencing organizational structures that enhance organizational survival and legitimacy.

This view of leadership emphasizes the relationship among incumbents of organizational roles. Here again, we find an argument against leadership as an individual quality and for leadership as a relationship. However, the relationship involves individuals who are in organizational roles. "Leadership flows through the networks of roles that comprise organizations" (Ogawa & Bossert, 1995, p. 225).

The influence at this systemic level occurs as individuals use their personal resources to influence others. These personal resources can include traits, expertise, and so forth needed by others to enact their role. Ogawa and Bossert (1995) illustrate the use of these resources: "In school organizations, district superintendents use their knowledge of state guidelines to influence school boards, principals, and teachers. Principals employ their knowledge of budgets to influence the decisions of both district superintendents and teachers on school councils. Also, teachers use their knowledge of effective instructional techniques to affect principals and district curriculum directors" (p. 235).

The personal resources used by individuals to influence others to whom they relate are not designated by formal position alone. While formal position may provide certain resources, those resources are hardly the only ones available within systems. Thus, influence and leadership can flow up and down (Katz & Kahn, 1966; Ogawa & Bossert, 1995; Tannenbaum, 1962). In this way, leadership becomes a systemic quality.

Systemic Leadership and Collaboration

Leadership as a systemic characteristic has obvious relevance for school collaboration, for example, teaming or collaboration across roles (see Pounder, chap. 5, Hart, chap. 6, this text). Through interaction among individuals in the same role and across roles, leadership flows throughout the organizational system. Leadership for collaboration involves individuals in various roles using their resources to meet each other's needs. Regular education teachers and special education teachers, for example, bring different resources to bear in the collaboration process and in so doing influence each other.

Yet leadership as systemic has implications for collaboration across organizational boundaries, for example, interagency collaboration. Individuals in social service organizations, for example, bring expertise, information, and resources to bear that are critically needed by teachers and principals to provide an appropriate education for students. In this relationship of roles, these individuals influence school staff. Of course, the direction of influence and thus leadership can work the other way as well.

LITERATURE ON LEADERSHIP
IN COLLABORATIVE SETTINGS

As mentioned above, few empirical studies exist that deal explicitly with leadership in collaborative settings. However, several recent studies on leadership regarding school reform can be useful for our understanding and for our later discussion of the promises and pitfalls of leadership in collaborative settings. This section begins with several studies of leadership that emphasize the expansion of leadership, both as to quantity and sphere. Then the section moves to consider several studies that investigate leadership for reform primarily from the school administrator's perspective. This discussion is intended not to be an exhaustive review but to be illustrative of the literature on leadership in reform settings.

Studies on the Expansion of Leadership Roles

Firestone (1996) uses two studies of change to illustrate a particular conception of leadership that is similar to the two features of leadership expansion in collaboration we have previously discussed. He argues that instead of defining leadership as what certain people do, we should define it as a set of functions that may be performed by various individuals in an organization. He identifies five leadership functions: providing and selling a vision, obtaining resources, providing encouragement, adapting standard operating procedures, and monitoring reform. Using Dolan-Dabrowski's (1992) study of the New Jersey State takeover of a school system and Heller's (1993) study of the institutionalization of a problem solving curriculum in eight schools, Firestone identifies the individuals/roles who perform these leadership functions. He found that many of these leadership functions are provided systemically, that is, by various people throughout the system. For example, monitoring improvement was done formally and informally by the principal, informally by teachers, and by state policy makers as well. In the same way, encouragement was provided by a variety of sources, including principals, teachers, district specialists, support staff, and trainers.

Firestone identifies three views of the school administrator's role in a "team model" of leadership in which functions are performed redundantly by more than one role. First, he suggests administrators "assess what is provided by others and offer what is missing" (p. 29). Second, administrators create a context where the leadership skills and potential of nonleaders are developed. Third, administrators commonly have the sole responsibility for representing the organization to the outside world.

Firestone's study is useful in helping to clarify leadership as systemic. Instead of focusing on the leadership behavior of one individual or role, his "team model" characterizes leadership in terms of functions performed by a variety of roles, sometimes singly and sometimes collectively.

In a similar way Pounder, Ogawa, and Adams (1995), using the conceptual framework described by Ogawa and Bossert (1995), examined the leadership exerted by various roles within the school context. They found that total leadership (the leadership exerted by all roles) is associated with school performance. However, they found that leadership functions in two organizational domains, the organization of work and commitment, and that "leadership in these two domains is provided by people in different roles" (p. 583). Specifically, they found that the leadership of principals and groups of teachers shape commitment, whereas parents' leadership is associated with student achievement through the organization of work. These authors conclude that "the leadership of people in different roles may affect different dimensions of school organization and thus different outcomes. This suggests that not all people should be expected to lead in all aspects of schools but should be involved in those aspects most pertinent to carrying out their roles" (p. 586).

Pounder et al. (1995) clarify leadership in ways that help us move away from a simplistic view of leadership expansion as "everyone becomes a leader." Their study clearly shows how leadership is provided by different roles for different organizational purposes. Principals and groups of teachers may influence commitment, but parents are more likely to influence student achievement.

Hart (1995) provides additional reinforcement for a more complex view of leadership expansion, especially in terms of teacher leadership. She identifies five purposes for teacher leadership: to further communitarian concerns, to use teacher expertise, to provide work design and incentives, to reform curriculum and instruction, and to promote a professional work environment. After examining alternative views of leadership that emphasize interactive, inclusive and reciprocal models and applying these to the strategies of mentor teachers, career ladders, and shared governance, she concludes, "Whatever the leadership teachers exercise or the expectations for outcomes other educators hold for teachers, planners, educators, and parents need explicitly to acknowledge that different goals and advantages are advanced by different features of teacher leadership structures" (p. 25).

Chrispeels (1992) conducted case studies of eight elementary schools in five different school districts in southern California. Her results led her to define instructional leadership in a way similar to the conception of leadership identified earlier in this chapter. She defines instructional leadership as "an influence relationship among principals, school staff, students, community, and district staff intended to bring about changes in the culture, school technology, and organization of the school so that there are significant and equitable achievement gains for all ethnic and income groups" (p. 140). One component of the effective schools she studied was shared leadership: "Leadership is not merely a component of an effective school but is the overarching and driving force that unites the school culture, school technology, and organizational structures in such a way to bring about enhanced student achievement" (p. 141).

Chrispeels's study also found evidence of systemic leadership: "The case study data indicate that leadership is needed at all levels—state, district, school site—and among all participants—state and district administrators, principals, and teachers—in order to achieve and maintain school improvement and effectiveness" (p. 145). She found that systemic leadership was created in part by the actions of principals in developing teacher leadership. In effective schools, principals were actively involved in nurturing the leadership of teachers. Nevertheless, Chrispeels also found that the leadership was reciprocal: "When the principal's leadership in the instructional and improvement roles was withdrawn, it was difficult for teacher leadership to sustain itself in these areas as well . . . [In] the least effective schools . . . in the absence of mechanisms that develop or encourage school-wide shared leadership, the leadership role of the principal appears to be made more difficult" (pp. 142–143).

Chrispeel's study highlights both features of the leadership expansion identified earlier. Her cases reflect a view of leadership as influence relationships within a systemic context. The reciprocal leadership she found was in part attributable to principals' work in developing others' leadership. Such a finding suggests the powerful role that leadership development plays not only in facilitating the expansion of leadership among others who are not in formal authority positions, but in facilitating the leadership of the formal authorities. Leadership development, far from decreasing the leadership of the principal or superintendent, may in fact increase it.

Fullan's (1990) work also suggests the systemic quality of leadership. Based on his team's research on a framework for change in schools, he concludes:

> We explicitly rejected the idea that leadership be a particular component of the framework. Leadership can, does, and must come from a variety of different sources. Any framework must allow for the fact that leadership critical for success comes from different sources in different situations (and different sources in the same situation over time). Leadership for success variously comes from the principal, key teachers, the superintendent, parents, trustees, curriculum consultants, governments, universities, etc. As the list reveals, the driving force for change can initially come from inside or outside the school, and from a variety of different roles. Once the model is fully functioning, leadership does indeed come from multiple sources simultaneously. (p. 16)

Fullan's conclusion reinforces the findings of the studies by Firestone, Pounder, Hart, and Chrispeel that leadership is systemic, not only because different individuals and roles are involved but because different functions are being provided by different individuals. The expansion of leadership, reflected in these studies, means that different individuals in and outside the system perform the same and different functions as they influence each other.

Studies of Leadership in School Reform Settings

Several studies investigate leadership occurring in different types of school reform settings. Most of these settings reflect restructuring agendas overall. The studies primarily look at the school administrator's perspective concerning leadership but suggest implications that we will identify in the next section.

Murphy (1994) identifies four role changes that have occurred for principals in restructured schools that should have relevance for our discussion of leadership for collaboration. First, he suggests that there has been a role change to "leading from the center." Based on Leithwood et al.'s (1992) study, this involves delegating leadership responsibilities and developing collaborative decision making processes in the school. Second, Murphy argues that enabling and supporting teacher success have become major leadership roles. This change involves such actions as helping to formulate a shared vision, cultivating a network of relationships, allocating resources consistent with the vision, providing information, and promoting teachers' development. Clearly most of these actions involve political behavior, for example, negotiating a shared vision and the allocation of resources. The third role change for leaders involves managing reform. The studies that Murphy reviews suggest that in restructuring schools, principals have taken on a more enhanced managerial role and a diminished instructional role. Any change in the role such as this involves a negotiation of interests as principals move from one role definition to another. Finally, Murphy argues that the role change has involved extending the school environment. Actions involving this role change include promoting the school, working with the governing board, and connecting with parents. Clearly these are activities that involve leaders in more systemic kinds of responsibilities.

Hallinger and Hausman (1994) suggest three possible roles for principals within the restructuring context: middle manager, instructional leader, and transformational leader. Yet their research found that "Despite the creation of new roles and decision-making structures, there is little evidence to suggest that the occupants of those roles have found satisfactory ways to share leadership responsibilities" (p. 172). Although managerial and instructional leadership adaptations have occurred, transformational leadership has not. These findings suggest the possible political nature of restructuring that principals may perceive. Sharing leadership not only involves changing the cultural norms of the organization but also involves political conflict.

This political nature of leadership is also found at the systemic level. Hallinger, Murphy, and Hausman (1992) in their study of principals' perceptions in restructuring schools found doubts raised by principals regarding the appropriateness of parent involvement in the restructuring movement: "Principals viewed the effects of restructuring on themselves almost exclusively in terms of power. They forecast new roles with fewer decisions to make by themselves as leading to a loss of control and power" (p. 335). These authors also found either an inability or reluctance by principals to let go of their experiences when developing visions of the future.

These authors also found that principals tended to interpret whatever they were currently doing as a form of restructuring. "Unconsciously perhaps, administrators are aware that it is easier to alter images than it is to transform cultural norms, organizational policies, and classroom practices. In certain locales, it may be enough to be known as a restructured school. This type of surface change alone may legitimate the school as a forward-looking institution of the 1990s" (p. 345).

Furthermore, the authors point out another leadership issue for principals in restructuring schools: accountability (see also Pounder, chap. 5, this text). Both hierarchical and nonhierarchical accountability dilemmas face these administrators: "Thus, both hierarchical and nonhierarchical accountability under shared decision making pose problems with which principals are unfamiliar and uncomfortable. A portion of their discomfort stems from their lack of confidence in other elements of the school system to adapt district policies and norms to support school-based accountability" (p. 347).

Another study reinforces the findings of Hallinger et al. Talbot and Crow (1996) in a recent study of Utah administrators found that the principals of Centennial schools (a restructuring model involving shared decision making and partnerships with external agencies) were slightly more likely than their non-Centennial counterparts to say they involve teachers and parents in school decisions. However, these differences were indeed small and were nonexistent when the issue involved the core technology of the school.

These last three studies emphasize that while the normative view of restructuring strategies such as collaboration may call for shared leadership, such a process is neither comfortable nor likely without political action. Much of the influencing that occurs in collaborative leadership may involve the negotiation of roles among participants. This does not have to mean that collaborative leadership cannot be developed, but it does mean that such leadership has a political quality.

Hess (1994) in his study of Chicago school reform efforts disagrees with the conclusions drawn by Murphy and by Hallinger and Hausman regarding the middle management role of principals. Hess argues that principals, at least in the Chicago setting, are no longer middle managers with responsibility to pass on the demands of superiors to subordinates. Rather he depicts principals as chief operating officers working with a managing board. "This means that principals are now accountable to their LSCs (Local School Councils) for the quality of staff coming into the school and for faculty performance. Their jobs depend on their abilities to motivate staff and to coordinate the school's educational program around a consistent theme or philosophy" (p. 64).

Hess's comments seem to ignore the political implications for principals of being in this type of leadership role. No doubt the human resources management and structural roles he identifies are present, but the accountability requirements make these actions very political as principals negotiate with both subordinates and local school council members regarding the "theme or philosophy" and what counts as quality.

Leithwood (1996) in a recent presentation on team learning—a significant issue for collaboration—identifies several leadership practices based on his study of transformational leaders: "group vision building and goal setting practices, the creation of collaborative cultures, setting high performance expectations, and providing psychological and material support for staff . . . (as well as) formal and informal strategies for stimulating staff members to think more reflectively and creatively about their work" (p. 20). He also suggests a direct leadership influence on team learning. "These studies describe school leaders facilitating the work of staff teams, for example, by ensuring that the knowledge of all members of the team is made explicit in team discussions and by encouraging innovative and coordinated action on the part of team members. In addition, these leaders also work to surface all members' interpretations of the problem(s) to be solved by the team and to develop, with the team, a clear as possible an interpretation of the problem(s)" (p. 20). Leithwood's findings suggest some specific leadership practices and resources necessary in the influence relationship we have described earlier. As Ogawa and Bossert (1995) suggest, resources such as information and expertise are critical power resources in the relationships that make up leadership. For parity and reciprocity to exist in collaborative setting, these leadership resources need to be available and shared in the explicit way Leithwood describes.

Conley (1993) in a study of schools involved in Oregon's restructuring program reinforces the critical role that information dissemination plays as a leadership function in these schools. In his study, principals took the role as disseminators of information, making sure that data is available to inform decisions and create visions. Conley also found that the principals were involved in allocating resources based on the shared vision of the school. He argues that allocating resources by using common focus as the criteria "replaces a process of resource allocation dominated by political considerations, what is commonly referred to as the 'squeaky wheel' method of management" (p. 81). However, this ignores the fact that developing a vision or a common focus is itself a political act in which various personal visions are negotiated into one or more collective visions.

Conley describes leadership in this regard: "This new style of leadership may have as its hallmark the ability of the leader to sublimate her or his ego to the collective needs and potentialities of the organization. This does not mean surrendering decision-making responsibility or adopting a laissez-faire style of leadership. It does suggest a very difficult balancing act requiring the principal to have a vision of education, but allowing that vision to be shaped and modified by others. The ultimate goal is to have one collective vision with broad ownership that incorporates elements of the principal's vision and of other members of the school community" (p. 329). Yet isn't this balancing act a political act?

The studies reported in this section suggest the dilemmas that school administrators face in leadership relationships in collaborative settings. Bredeson's (1993) study of school administrators in restructuring schools refers to the "role strain" that administrators face. This role strain appears as feelings of loss of control, uncertainty, fear of failure, and so forth. Peterson and Warren (1994) refer to the role uncertainty that principals face in these settings and the resulting changes in the political dynamics. Leadership for collaboration, far from being a peaceful, typically rational process, is full of discomfort, ambiguity, and uncertainty for school administrators. This process and its implications for school administrators in collaborative settings must be acknowledged for leadership in collaborative settings to work.

PROMISES AND PITFALLS OF LEADERSHIP FOR COLLABORATION: IMPLICATIONS FOR SCHOOL ADMINISTRATORS

The previous two sections lead to an understanding of the promises and pitfalls of leadership in collaborative settings and the resulting implications for school administrators. This section is organized according to the two primary features of the conception of leadership described earlier in the chapter: leadership as an influence relationship and leadership as systemic.

Leadership as an Influence Relationship: Promises and Pitfalls

Probably the most significant promise of collaboration in regard to leadership is that it has the potential for expanding leadership opportunities, resources, and benefits to more people. Such an expansion means that formal authority is not the only source for leadership. If leadership can be expanded to include teachers, parents, and even students, the possibilities for change ought to be greater.

However, since leadership involves an influence relationship, such an expansion increases costs such as time, effort, and other resources that are necessary for an influence relationship to work. If these leadership transactions result in a loss of resources for transactions associated with the core technology of the school, teaching and learning, we may doubt the worth of expanding leadership. Thus far research has not investigated these costs.

School administrators in collaborative settings must determine how to reduce the costs inherent in expanding leadership. Although some initial resources may be expended in developing the leadership potential in teachers, parents, students, and so on, the long-term benefits may outweigh the costs as the leadership resources and benefits multiply. Training these individuals in various leadership skills is vital for this expansion to work without incurring undue costs and losing resources for the primary teaching and learning functions of the school.

Murphy (1994) and Hallinger and Hausman (1994) suggest that the school administrator's role changes in such restructuring strategies as collaboration. These role changes involve political negotiation. Although some of these changes may be useful for school improvement and comfortable for school administrators, others may create the role strain that Bredeson (1993) describes. For example, if these authors are correct and the principal's role becomes more managerial and less instructional, it is likely that some school administrators who entered the profession for its instructional features may resist such change. Time taken in negotiating role changes with teachers, district superiors, and others may take away from equally or more important tasks.

Accountability, a major pitfall of collaboration, has implications for leadership overall and the work of school administrators in particular. While the normative view is that collaboration makes everyone accountable, that has not necessarily been the effect. Guskey and Peterson (1995) consider it a major reason that we have not yet found that restructuring positively effects student outcomes. In the influence relationship of leadership, it is easy to imagine that accountability may be a major target for negotiation as different individuals attempt to reduce their accountability responsibilities and increase the accountability of others. School administrators have traditionally been held responsible for what happens in their schools even in collaborative settings, and districts have been reluctant to disperse accountability across the participants. In these cases, principals are likely to continue to be held accountable but in a less controllable environment.

School administrators at all levels must negotiate openly the accountability demands. If accountability requirements are not negotiated and dilemmas are not resolved, successful collaboration has little hope (see also Pounder, chap. 5, this text).

For individuals to share leadership, that is, to be able to influence each other, there must be some parity in the relationship. This is probably most important in terms of the possession of leadership skills. Collaboration demands that individuals develop skills such as group problem solving, negotiation, and reflection.

The school administrator is probably in the best position to facilitate the leadership development of teachers and others. Encouraging, supporting, training, informing, and so on are critical responsibilities for school administrators to use in developing the leadership potential of teachers, students, and parents. Furthermore, supporting teachers' collective vision is a profound act of followership.

A major task for those involved in collaboration is information processing and dissemination. Pounder's chapter 5 in this book describes the necessity for administrators to provide task relevant information to teachers especially about school/district policies, legal considerations regarding student management and instruction, and so forth. She also points out the need for teacher teams to have a clear understanding of their "decision authority zone" relative to that of school administrators. Such information is vital to the expansion of leadership. If the principal hoards this information, there is little chance that others can exert influence. Information is a vital power resource. Whether school administrators are willing to share this resource will largely determine the success of collaboration.

Leadership as Systemic: Promises and Pitfalls

Understanding leadership for collaboration as systemic also highlights promises and pitfalls. Again the most obvious promise of collaboration in this regard is that leadership resources are expanded throughout the school and beyond to its environment. As mentioned in the previous section, this has the potential of increasing the opportunities for change. Leadership as systemic means that, instead of relying on the resources—expertise, sensitivity, knowledge, and so on—of the organization, educators and students can benefit from the resources of environmental sources, for example, mental health agency personnel.

Nevertheless, this kind of expansion also has its pitfalls. Leadership as systemic may also increase costs. Here costs involve control and coordination issues that increase as the boundaries of the organization are pushed back. For administrators, this means sharing leadership with individuals and organizations that are outside the school's boundaries and the administrator's control. "Under cooperation no one agency controls the whole process. To be sure, this point is taken for granted in any program of collaboration. However, neither schools nor most other children's service providers are institutions in which control is shared with ease . . . A fallout of this concern for control is a reluctance to share problems of control with other professionals" (Crowson & Boyd, 1993, pp. 159–160). Crowson and Boyd also stress that when control is shared it tends to be only partial or fragmented, for example, role specific. For this to change, administrators must increase the degree and quality of communication among participants. Such communication has its costs in time, effort, and so forth.

Another cost for the school administrator of expanding leadership to other agencies is time. Firestone (1996) found that the leadership function of representing the school to outside agencies has no substitute. It is a major role of the school administrator, but such entrepreneurial activity takes time away from instructional and managerial tasks. School administrators may perceive these costs to be excessive in terms of the role changes they produce.

A promise of leadership as systemic in collaborative settings is the expanding involvement of parents and community members. Expanding leadership to these groups has the potential for improving student outcomes (Pounder, Ogawa, & Adams, 1995) and increasing parental and community resources to the school. Yet as some studies (e.g., Talbot & Crow, 1996) have found that principals in collaborative settings are reluctant to involve parents in substantive decisions of core technology, for example, curriculum selection. Principals and teachers may perceive that such an expansion of leadership may result in a loss of power for them in an area in which they have traditionally had autonomy. Such a zero-sum notion of power and leadership defeats the very purpose of collaboration.

However, if principals begin to recognize that parents possess power resources needed by the school, for example, clout with district administrators, they may be more willing to develop processes for parents to be involved in core technology decisions.

The leadership as systemic perspective also points out the tendency for schools and school administrators to define collaboration as anything the school does that supports legitimacy. As Ogawa and Bossert (1995) point out, from an institutional perspective, administrators may claim their school is collaborative in order to gain legitimacy from district, state, and community members without making any attempt to link their efforts to specific student outcomes. Such actions are encouraged by funding tied to the adoption of specific kinds of reforms, such as site-based management. Administrators may go through the motions to expand leadership beyond the organizational boundaries to legitimize the school in the presence of its community. For the same reasons that collaboration cannot be mandated, perhaps it should not be manipulated through funding.

CONCLUSION

The expansion of leadership roles inherent in collaboration holds promise for schools. Nevertheless, as this chapter has suggested, we must move beyond mere normative views of leadership for collaboration to understand the complexities of leadership in these settings. If as we have maintained leadership is an influence relationship and is systemic, the expansion of leadership roles necessary for collaboration involves practical issues that need resolution.

It is all well and good to say principals need to change their outdated views about control and power and share leadership with teachers, students, parents, community members, and others. Still, unless we understand the political and organizational implications of this and develop resources to respond to them, we are not likely to see it occur but in rare circumstances. In such cases the pitfalls may outweigh the promises.

REFERENCES

Barnard, C. (1938). *Functions of the executive*. Cambridge, MA: Harvard University Press.

Blase, J. J. (1989). The micropolitics of the school: The everyday political perspective of teachers toward open school principals. *Educational Administration Quarterly, 24*, 377–407.

Bredeson, P. (1993). Letting go of outlived professional identities: A study of role transition and role strain for principals in restructured schools. *Educational Administration Quarterly, 29*, 34–68.

Burns, J. M. (1978). *Leadership*. New York: Harper & Row.

Cartwright, D. (1965). Influence, leadership, control. In J. G. March (Ed.), *Handbook of organizations* (pp. 1–47). Chicago: Rand McNally.

Chrispeel, J. H. (1992). *Purposeful restructuring: Creating a culture for learning and achievement in elementary schools*. New York: Falmer Press.

Conley, D. T. (1993). *Roadmap to restructuring: Policies, practices and the emerging visions of schooling*. Eugene, OR: ERIC Clearinghouse on Educational Management, University of Oregon.

Crow, G. A., Matthews, L. J., & McLeary, L. (1996). *Leadership. A relevant and realistic role for principals*. Princeton, NJ: Eye on Education.

Crowson, R. L., Boyd, W. L. (1993). Coordinated services for children: Designing arks for storms and seas unknown. *American Journal of Education, 101*, 140–179.

Dolan-Dabrowski, M. (1992). *A case study of the first year of state control of the Jersey City public schools*. Unpublished doctoral dissertation, Rutgers, State University of New Jersey, New Brunswick.

Firestone, W. A. (1996). Leadership: Roles or functions? In K. Leithwood et al. (Eds.), *International handbook of educational leadership and administration*. London: Kluwer.

Fullan, M. (1990). Staff development, innovation, and institutional development. In B. Joyce (Ed.), *Changing school culture through staff development* (pp. 3–25). Alexandria, VA: Association for Supervision and Curriculum Development.

Guskey, T. R., & Peterson, K. D. (1995, April). *School based shared decision making: The road to the classroom.* Paper presented at the annual meeting of the American Educational Research Association, San Francisco, CA.

Hallinger, P., & Hausman, C. (1994). From Attila the Hun to Mary had a little lamb: Principal role ambiguity in restructured schools. In J. Murphy & K. Seashore-Lewis, *Reshaping the principalship. Insights from transformational reform efforts* (pp. 154–176). Thousand Oaks, CA: Corwin Press.

Hallinger, P., Murphy, J., & Hausman, C. (1992). Restructuring schools: Principals' perceptions of fundamental educational reform. *Educational Administration Quarterly, 28,* 330–349.

Hart, A. W. (1995). Reconceiving school leadership: Emergent views. *Elementary School Journal, 96,* 9–28.

Heller, M. F. (1993). *Leadership functions in the implementation of planned change in the elementary school.* Unpublished doctoral dissertation, Rutgers, State University of New Jersey, New Brunswick.

Hess, G. A. (1994). New roles under school-based management: The Chicago school reform act. In R. J. Yinger & K. M. Borman (Eds.), *Restructuring education: Issues and strategies for communities, schools, and universities* (pp. 55–72). Cresskill, NJ: Hampton Press.

Katz, D., & Kahn, R. L. (1966). *The social psychology of organizations.* New York: Wiley.

Kelley, R. E. (1992). *The power of followership: How to create leaders people want to follow and followers who lead themselves.* New York: Doubleday.

Leithwood, K., Jantzi, D. Silins, H., & Dart, B. (1992, January). Transformational leadership and school restructuring. *Paper presented at the International Congress for School Effectiveness and Improvement.* Victoria, BC, Canada.

Leithwood, K. (1996). Doing business in restructuring schools: What is team learning anyway? In J. Burdin (Ed.), *1996 Yearbook of the National Council of Professors of Educational Administration.* Lancaster, PA: Technomic.

Mergendoller, J. R. (1981). *Mutual inquiry: The role of collaborative research on teaching in school-based staff development.* San Francisco: Far West Laboratory for Educational Research and Development.

Murphy, J. (1994). Transformational change and the evolving role of the principal: Early empirical evidence. In J. Murphy & K. Seashore-Lewis, *Reshaping the principalship. Insights from transformational reform efforts* (pp. 20–53). Thousand Oaks, CA: Corwin Press.

Ogawa, R. T., & Bossert, S. T. (1995). Leadership as an organizational quality. *Educational Administration Quarterly, 31,* 224–243.

Peterson, K., & Warren, V. (1994). Changes in school governance and principals' roles: Changing jurisdictions, new power dynamics, and conflict in restructured schools. In J. Murphy & K. Seashore-Lewis, *Reshaping the principalship: Insights from transformational reform efforts* (pp. 3–19). Thousand Oaks, CA: Corwin Press.

Pounder, D. G., Ogawa, R. T., & Adams, E. A. (1995). Leadership as an organization-wide phenomena: Its impact on school performance. *Educational Administration Quarterly, 31*(4), 564–588.

Rost, J. C. (1991). *Leadership for the twenty-first century.* New York: Praeger.

Talbot, D., & Crow, G. M. (1996). Comparing centennial and traditional principals: Demographics, attitudes and practices. In P. Galvin & D. Sperry (Eds.), *The conditions of Utah's public school leaders, 1995–96.* Salt Lake City, UT: The Utah Education Policy Center, University of Utah.

Tannenbaum, A. S. (1962). Control in organizations: Individual adjustment and organizational performance. *Administrative Science Quarterly, 7,* 236–257.

Thompson, J. D. (1967). *Organizations in action.* New York: McGraw-Hill.

Yukl, G. (1994). *Leadership in organizations* (3rd ed.). Englewood Cliffs, NJ: Prentice-Hall.

CHAPTER 9

Implications for Collaborative Educator Preparation and Development: A Sample Instructional Approach

Joe Matthews

As a high school principal wanting to change my bureaucratic ways to be on the cutting edge of innovation, I remember well my first attempt at establishing a collaborative ethic among the faculty in the suburban high school setting I was assigned. Having recently attended a site-based management workshop, I wanted to start the school year differently and have teachers establish a stronger voice in the administration of the school. I spent several summer weeks preparing for the first faculty meeting. My plans included establishing circles of chairs in the cafeteria where the faculty could sit together in teams and have a round table discussion on important issues that I had established on the agenda.

As the day finally came, teachers took their places in the circles to begin the collaborative effort. I wanted to take on the role of facilitator, introducing topics and then walking around to each circle, observing the activity and absorbing the ideas being presented. As the discussion opened and I started walking around, I was amazed at how little was being discussed. For the most part the groups were completely stymied. As I came to each group, they looked to me to join in with the discussion, much as they had seen me fill my role in years past. Soon I was doing most of the talking. When the lunch hour finally arrived, I was exhausted and both the teachers and I were greatly relieved. It was one of the longest mornings I ever had. The teachers filed into the faculty room where "the Colonel" had arrived with prepared chicken lunches.

Drained emotionally and physically from the morning's ordeal, I eventually walked into the faculty room to get my boxed lunch and join the faculty. As I was seating myself with a couple of teachers, I looked up amazed. The room was alive with conversation. Teachers were seated around tables, some were in couches, and others were standing as they were enthralled in discussion of the new school year.

Here, in the faculty room, with chicken leg in hand, was the real collaborative effort. Together again after a long summer vacation, these teachers were engaged in talking about real issues that affected them. My agenda was of less importance to them, perhaps even of no importance. My formal setting of circles of chairs in the cafeteria had stifled their discussion. I realized then that I had a lot to learn about establishing a collaborative effort in a school.

As I observed in my first attempt at forming faculty teams and in others since, collaborative efforts do not come naturally in many school settings. In fact, school practice historically has inhibited good collaborative efforts. Schools have been involved in a bureaucratic regime where open discussion and sharing of opinions, ideas, and ideology often have been discouraged and even stifled. When the time arrived for educators to be more democratic, become more involved in the decision-making process, collaborate with each other on curriculum and instruction, and cooperate more with parents and community, many educators were at a loss to make it happen (see also Pounder, chap. 5, this text).

As Johnson noted in an earlier chapter, several reasons appear to account for the growing interest in collaborative efforts in schools. He argued that the collaborative effort is rooted in our American political ideology, namely, the democratic ideal. Furthermore, decentralization in organizations is being viewed by many analysts as a means for increasing organizational productivity. Thus, site-based decision making and shared governance in schools have come to the fore. Additionally, special education, at-risk student teams, and instructional teams are more common and involve more educators in collaborative school efforts. Partnership practices between and among schools, businesses, and other agencies exemplify popular collaborative efforts involving groups external to the school. Beane and Apple (1995) advocated for "democratic schools" wherein all those directly involved in the school, including the students, have the right to participate in the process of decision making. "Committees, councils, and other schoolwide decision-making groups include not only professional educators, but also young people, their parents, and other members of the school community. In classrooms, young people and teachers engage in collaborative planning, reaching decisions that respond to the concerns, aspirations, and interests of both" (Beane and Apple, 1995, p. 9).

As these types of collaborative efforts become more prominent, the need for preparation and development of the personnel involved in collaboration also becomes more intense. In fact, educators and especially school leaders cannot go about doing what they have always done. As Hart outlined earlier in this book, all roles in the education process have been reconceputalized. The perceived traditional roles no longer exist.

These new roles for educators not only require a new way of thinking but also compel us to look at how we prepare and develop personnel in the profession. A new burden is upon those who plan and implement pre-service and in-service programs. Those who are involved with university preparation programs and staff development programs in school districts and state offices of education need to look at preparing educators, and especially school leaders, to acquire the skill development and practice needed for using the collaborative process. School collaboration has strong implications for the future development of insightful and collaborative educational leaders, not only as administrators but also as teachers, counselors, and other support staff.

Roland Barth (1990) observed that in the 1980s collaboration was seldom mentioned in the effective school literature. Indeed, the lack of emphasis on collaboration has greatly limited its use in America's schools. Consequently, there have been limited studies on the practice of collaborative efforts as part of the school reform movement. As Barth stated, "Collaboration appears to be neither part of the problem nor part of the solution when considering reform of public education" (p. v). Yet, there is growing evidence that collaborative efforts can and do make a difference in the education of our children. Barth continues his statement on collaborative efforts in schools by suggesting that school quality and collaboration go hand in hand and the need is greatly increasing for development of knowledge in collaborative practice:

> evidence is accumulating that the nature of the relationships among adults who live and work in schools has a tremendous influence upon the school's quality and character and on the accomplishment of its pupils. Two important tributaries feed this growing knowledge base: social science research, and the craft knowledge of teachers and principals. (p. v)

I hope to provide in this chapter a short rationale for the need for staff development and pre-service instructional courses in collaboration. I shall discuss university course and a staff development program in which I have been involved: it can provide a model or at least an example for others who are also interested in this pursuit. The course and program's purpose, the initial development of the course, the curricula and instructional methods and activities used in the course, and the resulting promises and pitfalls will be reviewed. The course has been in operation for eight consecutive years and much has been learned about its effectiveness. We have also learned a great deal about directions for planning and implementation in other settings. This course does not limit itself solely to a university setting. Indeed, rationale and examples will be provided for implementing the course in school staff development settings.

THE NEED FOR EDUCATOR PREPARATION
IN COLLABORATION SKILLS

As Pounder emphasized in chapter 5, several types of collaborative efforts appear in schools. Pounder listed three. The first type included groups such as management teams and school advisory committees. Management teams may include groups such as representative faculty and staff schoolwide teams, school site councils, districtwide administrative groups, and some elementary school grade-level teams. School advisory committees are established for advising school administrators concerning management responsibilities, such as school schedules, school hours, attendance areas, and new building needs. Some of these teams have now moved away from the advisory role and have taken over many management duties that were once part of the administrator's role. These site councils usually function as a part of site-based management and shared decision-making endeavors.

A second type of collaborative effort can be found in special services teams whose primary responsibility is to oversee and make decisions about exceptional children such as special education placement, programs for the gifted and talented, and at-risk children. Many of their responsibilities have been outlined through legal and legislated policy in developing and finding the best educational services for these students. Often these teams encompass more than just educators. They also include parents or surrogate parents and other service agency representatives.

Pounder identified a third type of team as the interdisciplinary instructional teams that emerged in the middle school movement. The interdisciplinary instructional team's chief responsibilities are to develop and implement curriculum and instructional techniques, coordinate interventions and management strategies, and to coordinate communication with parents.

Several variables affect the kind of collaborative decision-making and problem-solving efforts that can be made in such settings as outlined above. Among those variables are the preparation of the stakeholders in collaboration, the willingness of the stakeholders to collaborate and their commitment to the cause, the resources available, such as time and financial support, and the perceived merits of the collaborative effort. Perhaps, the one variable that is least understood and most over-looked is that of preparation of the stakeholders in the collaborative efforts. Indeed, collaboration in some circles is thought of as synony-mous with discussion and considered as something we can all do by just sitting around a table and talking. Unfortunately, there are those who believe that if we sit and talk long enough, some decision making will occur. They give little consideration to the skills which must be devel-oped to prepare those involved in the collaborative effort for the prob-lem-solving and decision-making process.

Questions need to be asked about what kind of preparation is nec-essary to develop the necessary group decision-making and problem-solving skills in school leaders, teachers, and other educators. Colleges, universities, or other pre-service preparation institutions that have the responsibility for developing preservice teachers, special educators, counselors, and school leaders must also respond to similar questions. What should be included in their programs that will better prepare edu-cators to meet the demand of collaborative efforts in schools?

Special consideration must be given to the preparation and develop-ment of building level and district level school leaders. Goldring and Rallis (1993) identified five forces that have emerged that have affected principals and their new role. These forces are: (1) teachers are becom-ing teacher-leaders; (2) student bodies are becoming more diverse, with variant needs; (3) parents are becoming more vocal and action-oriented advocates; (4) the social and technological contexts of schools are becoming more complex; (5) federal and state governments are mandat-ing restructuring activities and standards. Although educators can dodge these forces temporarily, doing so only will place both the school and the principal in peril.

Many (Hoy & Miskel, 1996; Tarter, Hox, & Kottkamp, 1990) have written on the role of the principal as a key element in establishing the climate of the school. Not only do collaborative efforts rely on the sup-port of the principal but, to work most effectively, an environment must exist in which collaborative efforts are promoted and individuals are developed. As Crow indicated in chapter 8, the school administrator is in the best position to encourage the leadership development of teachers. Quoting Crow (p. 205), "Encouraging, supporting, training, and informing are critical responsibilities to use in developing the leadership potential of teachers, students and parents." Therefore, it is imperative that principals have training in using and helping others use collabora-tive methods. The reality is that other educators in the school respond directly or indirectly to what the principal does or does not do. No other single role in a school building has as much potential influence on the collaborative climate as does the principal's. The principal's modeling of collaboration not only can set a positive tone but also may establish a precedent for other educators to accept their responsibility for learning and using collaboration. Rosenholtz (1989) found that schools characterized by a high degree of social interaction between teachers and the principal were also characterized by a high degree of cooperation among teachers. In other words, when the principal plays the music, the teachers seem to join in with the dance.

The district administrators can also promote collaborative efforts and do so through various means. First, district administrators can seek to hire personnel with training and experience in collaboration. As more training opportunities emerge for pre-service candidates in collaboration, district personnel will need to emphasize the importance of this training to future employees. Second, district administrators can effectively place educators in buildings to promote collaborative efforts, giving those with less experience opportunities to work with those with more experience. Building principals who have had both training and experiences in collaborative efforts need to be placed with faculties who have desire and need for collaboration. Third, district administrators can plan, implement, and support staff development opportunities for district employees. District administrators need to do much more than encourage collaboration. They must help make it happen. Providing the resources necessary for implementing staff development programs for all educators can make a difference in the direction and degree of collaborative efforts in the schools. If we believe that principals need to carry the torch and lead their respective faculties into collaborative efforts, then we have to provide the training necessary for them to use the collaborative process.

COURSE DEVELOPMENT AND DESCRIPTION

To meet the growing need for educators trained in the collaboration process, the Graduate School of Education at the University of Utah developed, through a collaborative effort among four departments, a course for preparing professionals for educational partnerships, teaming and collaborative efforts in decision making and problem solving. The departments of Educational Administration, Educational Studies, Educational Psychology, and Special Education joined resources and developed a graduate-level course targeted for pre-service and in-service educators, namely, teachers, special educators, school counselors, school psychologists, and school administrators. Since the inception of the course, a staff development program has emerged for schools to train and develop inservice school personnel.

The Collaborative Educational Problem Solving and Conflict Management course was originally developed in 1988 by six faculty members of the Graduate School of Education at the University of Utah. The course presently is taught by four faculty members, one representative from each of the four departments in the Graduate School of Education. The course was originally designed to meet for two to three hours weekly in a ten-week quarter system. The course was designed to have equal enrollment by students from all educator roles, that is, classroom teachers, special education teachers, school counselors, school psychologists, and school administrators. However, a true balance was never fully expected or realized. Specifically, pre-service and in-service regular classroom teachers consistently have been under represented in the course.

Since the course's original implementation, a modification occurred that has enhanced the quality of the experience. The course has been changed from the weekly class format held over an entire term to a one week intensive workshop format held during the summer. The reasons for the change were twofold. First, the one-week summer course better accommodates in-service educators who are practicing in the field. This change has greatly increased the number of teachers enrolled in the course. Second, the instructors felt that the one-week format encouraged better team building and team collaboration practice. Without the interruption of other activities during a term, teams bond better and manage team processes more efficiently. We felt the students learned the collaboration concepts more effectively and efficiently.

COURSE OBJECTIVES AND CURRICULA

Three elements in particular act as integral parts of the curricula for the course: (1) collaborative problem solving and decision making, (2) group dynamics and processes, and (3) conflict management. As indicated by Welch, et al. (1992, p. 3), the co-founders of the course, "Our primary intent was to provide students with a unique interdisciplinary training experience, wherein the elements of collaboration, problem solving, shared decision making, and conflict management could be operationalized and practiced in simulated role-play activities."

The present course objectives are to:

1. Understand the role and function of educational personnel within a school system

2. Learn intervention strategies and skills involved in team problem solving

3. Understand and apply a collaborative model of problem solving

4. Gain experience in collaborative problem solving with specific school related problems

5. Learn communication skills and practice them within the context of your class team

6. Understand the principles of group dynamics and learn conflict management strategies

7. Assess one's own interaction style in group settings and refer to it throughout the course

A model of the conceptual knowledge used in the course is presented in figure 9.1. Using the metaphor of building blocks, the six concepts of knowledge are (1) understanding group dynamics and mechanics, (2) understanding the traditional and the newly conceptualized roles of educators in the collaborative environment, (3) understanding collaborative problem solving, (4) learning to manage conflict, (5) learning interpersonal communication skills, and (6) learning the collaborative ethic (figure 9.1).

Understanding the Roles and Functions of Educational Personnel

An essential part of the course is the discussion of the changing roles of educational personnel. Traditional and reconceptualized roles of the school principal, counselor, school psychologist, special education teacher, and regular education teacher are examined. Each role is reviewed from a traditional perspective based on cultural and societal expectations. Each role is further reviewed from a newly conceptualized

FIGURE 9.1
The Building Blocks of Collaborative Conceptual Knowledge

framework. Hart describes in chapter 6 the concepts, functions, and evolving nature of roles in the educational setting and describes the aspects of the newly conceptualized roles.

Role identification and analysis are important concepts in learning about collaboration. We have found that most of our participants have very real and often biased preconceptions about various educator roles. Breaking down these perceptual biases is a difficult process, one that takes more than just a university course or a staff development program. However, the initial steps are taken, and progress can be seen as students learn more about the dynamic, change oriented, concept of the roles. Students gain a deeper sensitivity toward the role preconceptions that often create barriers for collaborative teams.

Understanding the Collaborative Ethic

The definition and description of collaboration in educational settings is discussed early in the course. It is introduced as a framework for educational problem solving. As Welch et al. (1992) describe it, educational collaboration is a dynamic process, not an end product or a static state. Friend and Cook (1990) define the collaborative ethic as a set of values or principles that endorse collegial versus independent action as professionals voluntarily work together to make decisions and solve problems in schools.

Team Building and Understanding Group Dynamics

Early in the course, participants are placed in teams. As instructors, we assign each participant in a team to the professional role they currently hold or aspire to hold. We also consider a mix of age and gender in team placement. Teams include five to seven members, and each team has at least one school counselor, one school psychologist, one school administrator, and one or two special education teachers and regular classroom teachers. As indicated earlier, we typically have had fewer participants in regular classroom teachers than in other roles. Often we ask school counselors and administrators to fill the role of classroom teacher if they have had experience in that role.

The teams begin collaborating when they are formed. We assign certain ice-breaking activities to help the team members get to know each other and to bond together. One example of these bonding activities is to assign the teams to go out to lunch together on the first day. This often brings some anxiety to the participants since they usually have other plans. Some participants have brought sack lunches and have not brought money for a lunch. We simply ask the team to work out a plan with each individual in mind so that all team members can participate.

Effective collaboration requires several skills, some of which are the sharing of resources and the understanding of other stakeholders on the team. We have felt this one activity has done more than any other in the shaping and bonding of the team members. Without exception, this bonding activity has brought the team members together and has initiated a dynamic for future collaborative activities. Quite often the teams continue going out to lunch for the duration of the workshop.

An important component of teaming is to understand the interpersonal styles that participants possess. We help participants analyze their own personal styles and how those styles affect the total group process. Two key ingredients are introduced in analyzing personal style: cooperation and assertiveness (Friend and Cook, 1992). Participants analyze the degree of cooperativeness and assertiveness they normally exhibit in a group process. We then direct a discussion of how these elements affect the collaborative process. For example, a team member with too little cooperativeness and too much assertiveness is often viewed by other team members as possessing a competitive, aggressive style. Likewise, a team member with little cooperativeness and little assertiveness is often perceived as not involved and apathetic. Understanding individual styles as they affect the group and the collaborative process is an important element in the participants' development.

Understanding and Applying a
Collaborative Model of Problem Solving

We emphasize a systematic approach to team collaborative problem solving. Hart described in chapter 6 the collaborative models of problem solving, largely rational linear models. We incorporate important concepts from these models in forming the conceptual knowledge base for the students. We use the models as frameworks for collaborative problem-solving activities involving case studies from real school situations. Problem identification and definition is the first step and the problem solving process continues through the solution stages and plan implementation. Hart described the collaborative problem-solving process in detail in chapter 6.

The most important part of the collaborative problem-solving process, yet one which is often given minimal attention by participants, is problem identification. When teams practice the process with case studies, most often participants identify the problem as being of a global nature and it becomes unsolvable. We spend considerable time coaching the teams about problem identification, focusing on one problem component that can be solved. We ask the team to write the problem definition on paper so that it is clear and concrete to all team members.

Early in the course, teams often do not get any further than problem identification in the time alloted for the case study exercise. Although the team members feel they have failed in adequately solving the case study problem, we feel otherwise. It is important to learn to correctly identify the problem. We relate to the participants experiences in which school teams have felt like they have solved the problem only to find out that the problem they solved is quite different from the real problem.

Teams also tend to move too quickly to the solution stage without proper brainstorming. At the beginning stages, teams will often finish much earlier than expected, claiming they have reached the solution and implementation stage. Further analysis on the part of the instructors usually reveals that the solution was arrived at prematurely. The selected solution often does not address the defined problem. The team did not spend enough time in seeking all possible solutions. This often occurs when one member of the team dominates the discussion and moves his or her own agenda forward.

Considerable discussion is given to brainstorming. Brainstorming for solutions requires the team to generate as many ideas as possible, think creatively, withhold qualitative judgements of alternatives, and use active listening (Welch et al., 1992). The brainstorming process usually improves as team members learn to be more assertive. As the course progresses, seldom do teams go through the solution process too rapidly. We hope students learn that the process of successful collaborative problem solving does take time, does involve considerable understanding of other team members, and does require management of conflict. Students often claim that when the solution stage is finished and the implementation plan is devised, the collaborative solution and plan are better than they had originally thought.

At the beginning of the course we allow teams to use a worksheet with the problem solving steps outlined. As the course develops, the teams wean themselves from the written guidelines. The students internalize the logic of the problem-solving process after they use it a few times. We recommend that each group have a facilitator who will keep the team on task and following the steps. We do suggest, however, that the process steps be used not as a recipe but, rather, as a guide to keep the group moving in the right direction. Even the best of groups tend to digress. A good facilitator allows the group to communicate freely but also directs them toward the task at hand.

Although the clinical nature of the course does not allow for plan implementation, we do explain to the students the necessity of remaining involved with a team during the implementation and evaluation stages. The instructors emphasize a data-based, decision-making process for evaluation.

Understanding Conflict Management

A strength of collaboration is that participants bring diverse backgrounds, experiences, and knowledge to problem-solving situations. However, participant roles also bring different expectations and demands. Power struggles often emerge as participants protect their own turf, promote ideas, and defend past practices. Interaction in collaborative efforts brings conflict, and that conflict threatens the collaborative process. A fundamental component of the developmental process in collaboration is to learn how to manage conflict and use it as a force of strength and progress rather than as a detriment. Participants need to understand that conflict is inevitable and that the manner in which we handle the conflict determines whether it becomes constructive or destructive (see also Barott & Raybould, chap. 3; Galvin, chap. 4; Hart, chap. 6, this text).

In teaching conflict management skills, we use the five collaborative management styles that are determined along the dimensions of assertiveness and cooperativeness as presented by Friend and Cook (1992) and Johnson and Johnson (1991). They include competitive, accommodating, avoiding, compromising, and collaborative styles. To manage conflict in collaborative efforts, participants must choose to use one of the five styles. We attempt to show how each style has an effect on the collaborative process.

A *competitive* style is characterized by high assertiveness but low cooperativeness. A participant who uses this style often is perceived by others as being overpowering or aggressive. Johnson and Johnson (1991) characterized this style as that of a shark. Getting what they want is more important than developing relationships with those involved.

An *accommodating* style is typified by low assertiveness but high cooperativeness. A person using this style of conflict management often seeks harmony with others above his or her own goal attainment. Johnson and Johnson (1991) symbolized this style as that of a "teddy bear"— seeking relationships is more important than seeking personal goals.

Those using *avoiding* styles are symbolized as "turtles" (Johnson and Johnson, 1991). They hide from conflict. They are neither cooperative nor assertive. They do not pursue their own goals, nor do they pursue establishing relationships with others. They often will put up a "good face" disguising or minimizing the conflict. This is a dangerous style in education since it often depicts a person as being "helpless and hopeless."

People with *compromising* styles of conflict management are seeking the middle ground. They achieve a limited degree of cooperativeness and assertiveness. Johnson and Johnson (1991) depicted them as being "foxes" because they sacrifice some of their own opinions and solutions and expect others to do the same. Compromise is often present in political circles where common ground is sought so that there is an appearance of something being accomplished.

A *collaborative* style of conflict management is characterized by high cooperativeness and high assertiveness. These persons value their relationship with others but also value their own goals. They will seek for even better relationships and for a better solution than their own. The symbol used by Johnson and Johnson (1991) for the collaboration style is the "owl."

We suggest that conflict is best managed by an "owl" approach. We illustrate from past examples how conflict can promote better collaboration because it involves people sharing more ideas and trying harder to find a better solution. However, as Welch and Sheridan (1995, p. 127) indicate, a collaborative style of conflict management does require both time and training.

Developing Interpersonal Communication Skills

Effective communication skills are essential in collaborative efforts. Although it seems obvious, it is an area that seldom receives much attention in preparing for collaborative activities. As part of our course we emphasize two important elements in interpersonal communication skills: active listening and relationship-building skills. Welch and Sheridan (1995) devised acronyms as teaching tools to help the students learn these communication skills. Active listening involves learning CAPS, i.e., clarifying, attending, paraphrasing, and summarizing. Relationship-building skills involves learning GRACE. i.e., genuineness, reflection, acceptance, concreteness, and empathy.

Course Methods and Activities

To help internalize the conceptual knowledge for the course, the students role-play collaborative problem-solving situations involving school scenarios. The teams are formed during the first session and remain intact throughout the course. The initial scenarios are quite simple, and we emphasize the systematic approach to problem solving—especially problem identification. As the course progresses, we introduce the students to other concepts that they in turn practice in their collaboration exercises. The case study problems progressively become more difficult so that more intense skill development can be practiced in problem solving, interpersonal communication, and conflict management.

After each problem-solving exercise, the team members evaluate their own personal participation and that of their team. Evaluation is based on the problem-solving process as well as other important skills. Individuals analyze their own personal styles during the collaborative exercises to evaluate how they could be more effective.

One facet of the team case study exercises is what we call the "fish bowl" sessions. In these sessions, a team working on a problem-solving activity will be observed and evaluated by another team. After the team problem-solving exercise, the observing team gives feedback on how the team functioned in a collaborative effort. This exercise provides development in two areas. First, the feedback given by peers is usually viewed as meaningful and deserving. It provides a "mirror" to the group, showing the team what they did well and what they could do better. Second, those giving the feedback integrate the necessary skills they have learned and apply them in their observation. This process substantially increases their own skills in knowing the collaborative problem-solving process.

Another important part of the developmental process in the course is journal writing. Students are assigned to write reflective entries in a journal on several topics: the conceptual knowledge that was presented, analysis and reflection on the individual and group processes, and a final reflection on how they plan to implement the learning in their particular roles and job assignments. After each concept is presented and discussed in class, we allow students to take fifteen minutes and reflect on the concept in their journals. Likewise, after the group process with the case studies, students are given fifteen minutes to reflect in writing on their participation and on their team's participation. The final reflection entry in the journal is an out-of-class assignment due one week after the end of the course. This writing exercise is expected to be more involved and more analytical. Students are to incorporate the conceptual knowledge and apply it to their particular roles in their present or expected assignments.

USING THE COURSE AS A
STAFF DEVELOPMENT PROGRAM

We have had the opportunity to use the course as a staff development program in a local elementary school. Several of the teachers in a local elementary school had previously taken our course and were familiar with it. As the school's faculty began looking into various innovative practices, all of which included teams and site-based decision-making committees, the teachers approached the principal and suggested our course become part of their staff development. From that origin, we collaborated and developed a program similar to our course outline. We then offered the program to those faculty members who chose to participate. The program was arranged in special staff development days prior to the new school year. Teachers were compensated for their involvement.

Instead of assigning groups as is done in the regular course, the teachers were placed in action teams that were given responsibilities to develop plans for real school improvement issues. As we began the program, we allowed the teams to go through the regular case study problem-solving activities to develop and practice needed collaborative skills. Toward the end of the program, we allowed the teams to begin actual collaboration on their action plans.

Based on experience, we concluded that the program worked equally well as a staff development program and as a unversity course. Subsequent observations have revealed that even though there have now been new teachers added to the faculty, the teachers who have been trained continue to use the skills developed in collaboration and they have helped the new teachers by serving as models and resources for help.

PROMISES AND PITFALLS OF TRAINING AND DEVELOPMENT PROGRAMS IN COLLABORATION

Establishing collaborative training and development opportunities for educators has its promises and pitfalls. We see promise in collaborative training: a number of previous students have returned and told us how much the course has helped them and their school collaborative efforts. One student was so enthusiastic about her involvement with teams at her school that she wanted to come to our subsequent summer class and tell others about her school's positive experience. As she testified about her own development, she credited the course as being the stimulus for her own instructional improvement team. She claimed she was a better teacher because she now collaborated with other faculty members on innovative practices. She substantiated Evans-Stout's (chap. 7) point that one is more willing to take risks if one need not do it alone (Stout citing Johnston, Markle, & Arhar, 1988). It is safer as a team to try innovative teaching methods.

The development of students in the course is also evident to observers. Students initially perceive collaborative problem solving as a means to determine a final solution rather than a process in which continual collaborative efforts produce more solutions. Students often are tenuous in their initial participation, but contribute more substantially as they learn to balance cooperativeness and assertiveness. Our observations also show that in the beginning of the course students often seek solutions before understanding the problem. As they develop more practice, collaborative efforts enlighten their problem understanding and solutions become more realistic.

One of the pitfalls of collaborative training is some students' resistance to the instructional methods used. Specifically, some students are quite uncomfortable in role-playing situations. Some have dropped out of the course when it became apparent that it not only involved acquiring conceptual knowledge but practicing using that knowledge. Those who stay most often lose their reluctance as they become more comfortable with the process.

The systematic steps used in the problem-solving process can be both a promise and a pitfall of collaborative training. For many students the steps are helpful in overcoming their own participation anxiety. They have a plan to work, an outline to follow. On the down side, the steps can be taken too literally or rigidly and used as a recipe or crutch. Some students rely so heavily on the problem-solving steps that it inhibits the natural progression of the collaborative effort. The steps need to be used initially so that the group follows a methodical process. However, as the group works together over a period of time, the process should become more natural and fluid.

Perhaps, our most difficult problem has been the communication and coordination of efforts required in an interdisciplinary program. There have been and continue to be certain barriers to overcome in the teaching process. These include faculty load, scheduling of faculty time and courses, and consistency among the faculty in expectations of student outcomes. Instructors have learned that considerable time and effort are required as a team; we expend as much or more time with this course as we do with courses we teach independently. To collaboratively teach this course, the instructors must deal with and practice the same collaboration skills that they are teaching to students. Nevertheless, comments from our students consistently indicate that our collaboration has been both an inspiration and a model for them to pursue collaborative efforts.

In conclusion, as instructors we have learned that preparing educators for collaborative efforts in schools is a challenging and promising cause. Many of our students have gone on to develop and prepare other educators in learning the skills of collaboration. Schools have adopted our model and have pursued better teaching and learning efforts through collaboration. We remain satisfied that our efforts have provided a systematic and practical instructional approach for developing collaborative educators.

REFERENCES

Barth, R. (1990). Foreword. In S. C. Smith & J. J. Scott, *The collaborative school: A work for effective instruction* (pp. v–vii). Eugene, OR: ERIC Clearinghouse on Educational Management and Reston, VA: National Association of Secondary School Principals.

Bean, J. A., & Apple, M. W. (1995). The case for democratic schools. In M. W. Apple & J. A. Bean (Eds.), *Democratic schools* (pp. 1–25). Alexandria, VA: Association for Supervision and Curriculum Development.

Friend, M., & Cook, L. (1990). Collaboration as a predictor for success in school reform. *Journal of Educational and Psychological Consultation, 1,* 69–86.

Friend, M., & Cook, L. (1992). *Interactions: Collaboration skills for school professionals.* New York: Longman.

Goldring, E. B. & Rallis, S. F. (1993). *Principals of dynamic schools: Taking charge of change.* Newbury Park, CA: Corwin Press.

Hoy, W. K., & Miskel, C. G. (1996). Educational administration: Theory, research and practice (5th ed.). New York: McGraw Hill.

Johnson, D. W., & Johnson, F. P. (1991). *Joining together: Group therapy and group skills* (4th ed.). Englewoods Cliffs, NJ: Prentice-Hall.

Johnston, J. H., Markle, G. C., & Arhar, J. M. (1988). Cooperation, collaboration, and the professional development of teachers. *Middle School Journal, 19*(4), 28–32.

Kelley, E. (1980). Improving school climate. Reston, VA: National Association of Secondary School Principals.

Rosenholtz, S. J. (1989). *Teacher's workplace: The social organization of schools.* New York: Longman.

Tarter, J., Hox, W. K., & Kottkamp, R. (1990). School health and organizational commitment. *Journal of Research and Development in Education, 23,* 236–243.

Welch, M., Sheridan, S. M., Fuhriman, A., Hart, A. W., Connell, M. L., & Stoddart, T. (1992). Preparing professionals for educational partnerships: An interdisciplinary approach. *Journal of Educational and Psychological Consultation, 3,* 1–23.

Welch, M., & Sheridan, S. M. (1995). *Educational partnerships: Serving students at risk.* Fort Worth, TX: Harcourt Brace.

CHAPTER 10

Promises and Pitfalls
of Collaboration:
Synthesizing Dilemmas

Diana G. Pounder

The preceding chapters have discussed many considerations regarding school collaboration using multiple disciplinary perspectives. These include: (1) organizational structure and change considerations informed by organizational theory; (2) costs and dynamics of exchange relationships informed by organizational economics; (3) educator work design and role considerations informed by social and organizational psychology; and (4) implications of collaboration for teaching and learning, school leadership, and professional preparation and development. Also, the book specifically discusses both interagency collaboration (Galvin, chap. 4) and collaboration among school professionals (Pounder, chap. 5, and Hart, chap. 6).

We now turn our attention to some key synthesizing issues or dilemmas that cut across these multiple perspectives and types of collaboration. These dilemmas will be framed as collaboration's promises versus pitfalls—or opportunities versus challenges for schools.

OPPORTUNITIES AND CHALLENGES
OF COLLABORATION

There are several synthesizing issues or dilemmas that present important opportunities and challenges for those who engage in collaborative school efforts. These dilemmas include: (1) the need for change toward more collaborative schools versus the persistence of schools, (2) resource gains versus costs of collaboration, (3) professional interdependence versus profes-

174 RESTRUCTURING SCHOOLS FOR COLLABORATION

sional autonomy or discretion (and the related concepts of independence, privacy, and isolation), (4) shared influence (or leadership) versus shared accountability (or responsibility), and (5) balance of influence versus over-control or underinvolvement among collaborative parties.

The Need for Collaborative Change
versus the Persistence of Schools

There are many reasons that schools may desire or even need to become more collaborative. Johnson (see chap. 2) introduces two commonly touted reasons for increasing collaboration in schools: (1) to increase the democratization of schools, and (2) to enhance school effectiveness and/or productivity. Galvin (see chap. 4) discusses historical events and trends that have influenced schools to become more collaborative with other agencies. These events include the 1980s calls for reform to address our "failing" education system and a corresponding crisis in America's social services, struggling to effectively meet the growing needs of children and families plagued by poverty, unemployment, violence, homelessness, teen-age pregnancy, and other social welfare problems. Pounder (see chap. 5) argues that increased collaboration among teachers and professional educators can tighten the connection between educators' work and student outcomes, especially increasing educators' comprehensive knowledge and responsibility for students' learning and school experiences. Organizing and designing work around students may increase student learning, achievement, and other valued school outcomes. Correspondingly, students' fractionalized school experience and sense of detachment or alienation from school may be decreased. Also, collaborative work approaches, moreso than individual job enhancement, may enrich educators' work and increase involvement across all educators without violating the norms of egalitarianism so prevalent among school professionals. Hart (see chap. 6) reenforces the argument that increased collaboration can improve student outcomes and school effectiveness. She reminds us that students' needs are becoming increasingly complex due to the greater number of special needs students and to the greater cultural diversity of the student body. This increased complexity necessitates greater collaboration and sharing among education professionals who possess varied and complementary expertise. Evans-Stout (chap. 7) traces the reasoning that collaboration may enhance student learning by changing the instructional process and the way teachers work. However, she points out that research findings largely emphasize the effect of instructional collaboration on teachers' work lives. Only a few recent studies have explored and found favorable relationships between instructional collaboration, teachers' learning and work lives, and enhanced student learning (e.g., Smylie, Lazurus, and Brownlee-Conyers, 1996).

In spite of these and other reasons for schools to become more collaborative, Evans-Stout (see chap. 7) and Barott and Raybould (see chap. 3) remind us of the "sameness"—the stability, persistence, even inertia of schools. That is, schools are notoriously slow or even resistant to change. Barott and Raybould explain the nature of change, types of change, and the paradoxical relationship between change and persistence. It is this persistence, or inertia, that Stout describes when addressing the stability of instructional methods used in schools for decades. There are many reasons that schools persist in their instructional methods, organizational structure, work roles, and general operating dynamics. The book's authors have addressed some of these reasons, several of which are discussed in greater detail below as key dilemmas for collaborative schools. One such factor that strongly contributes to schools' persistence is the norm of autonomy or independence that runs counter to norms of collaboration (see chapters by Johnson, Barott and Raybould, Hart, Pounder, and Evans-Stout). This autonomy or privacy norm is often reenforced by professional training and socialization (Matthews, chap. 9, Hart, chap. 6). Also identified are the dynamics of exchange relationships, including costs (e.g., coordination, communication, monitoring) incurred while collaborating (Galvin, chap. 4). If collaboration increases organizational costs and complexity unduly, especially in an environment noted for its stimulus overload (Johnson, chap. 2), educators could be expected to resist more collaborative work relationships. Also, because schools have needs to be buffered from their environment, there will always be clear limits to the ways or degree to which schools will collaborate with (or bridge) external agencies or parties (Ogawa, 1996, as cited by Johnson, chap. 2, and Barott and Raybould, chap. 3). Further, some types of collaboration may require far-reaching and thorough organizational change. If existing incentives, rewards, and organizational structures run counter to collaborative work dynamics and objectives, schools will persist in their traditional ways of operating.

This tension between needs for collaborative school change and the stability or persistence of schools presents a dilemma for those considering collaborative endeavors. Developing a more collaborative school demands careful negotiation and navigation of the change process and is unlikely to be worth the effort unless the collaborative endeavors are organized around the core technology of schools—the teaching-learning process. Collaboration efforts that are largely symbolic may reflect our democratic ideals but are unlikely to result in substantive improvement in school and student outcomes.

Resource Gains versus Costs of Collaboration

The book's authors discuss a range of benefits and costs associated with collaboration. Many of the benefits could be characterized as resource gains. These gains include resources such as increased expertise, knowledge, and skills available for shared educational problem-solving. Also, the efforts of more personnel, with a greater array of information and perspectives, may be available to address student learning or related concerns. Interagency collaboration can also increase fiscal resources available to the cooperating agencies, resources such as shared facilities, equipment, or personnel. These combined resource gains promise to enhance school effectiveness.

However, these resource gains may be offset by the costs associated with increased collaboration. These costs include increased time and effort associated with joint planning, communication, coordination, and monitoring of complex collaborative programs and processes. (Galvin's chapter offers significant detail about the nature of costs associated with collaboration.) These costs can contribute to inefficiencies in achieving educational goals and objectives. Inconsistent or inadequate commitment, input, and information among collaborative parties can further compromise the effectiveness and/or efficiency of shared efforts.

In sum, the gains in school effectiveness promised by school collaboration may be compromised by the costs or inefficiencies that can occur with collaboration. Those initiating collaborative programs or functions must give serious consideration to organizing structures and processes that minimize the costs that can kill collaborative efforts. In other words, collaboration leaders must consistently consider how to reduce "hindrance" factors such as unclear goals and expectations, unproductive meetings, complicated communication patterns, complex coordination plans, or excessive paperwork, documentation, or other costly monitoring functions. Leaders must explore ways to capture the rewards of collaborative work without making the work too difficult, time consuming, or frustrating to accomplish.

Professional Interdependence versus Professional Autonomy

Repeatedly this book's authors have referred to an important contextual consideration for school collaboration—the existing culture and norms of schools and education professionals. Discussions of the norm of professional autonomy or discretion, often associated with professional independence, privacy, or isolation have been particularly prevalent. Although educators and researchers often lament the isolation associated with teaching, professional isolation is only one side of the professional autonomy coin. That is, as much as teachers may embrace collaboration to reduce professional isolation, they also fear the loss of professional discretion, independence, and privacy. Collaboration necessitates a certain professional interdependence in planning, decision making, delivery of instruction and services, and other important aspects of educators' work.

As introduced earlier (see chap. 5), collaboration brings greater professional interdependence among individuals. However, collaboration can allow, encourage, or even necessitate increased autonomy and discretion as a group or collaborative unit. Instructional options, service provisions, or decision influences that are unavailable to educators as individuals may be more commonplace or "do-able" in collaborative work groups. In other words, collaboration may reduce *individual* autonomy (and individual discretion, privacy, and isolation) but increase *group* autonomy or discretion.

Educators engaging in school collaboration efforts may initially fail to realize the full potential of collaborative groups to exercise greater freedom, independence, or discretion in their decision making and choices of action. To attain this group autonomy, members must establish new work paradigms—brainstorm new ways for achieving their instructional and educational objectives. Through new work methods and organizational arrangements, educators may come to appreciate the discretion available to them as group members. Professional interdependence may be appreciated in spite of some reduction of individual independence or privacy. And the corresponding reduction in feelings of professional isolation would probably be appreciated by most teachers.

Shared Influence versus Shared Accountability

Collaborative schools tend to expand decision influence and leadership to teachers and other organizational members, and they can also extend influence to others outside the school such as parents, external agency members, or other community participants. The dynamics of shared influence and leadership have been a popular focus of research during the past few years, especially as shared leadership relates to restructured schools (see Crow, chap. 8, for an extensive discussion of this literature). However, there has been limited discussion of the accountability or responsibility that necessarily must correspond to broadened leadership or influence by teachers and others.

As teachers and other school employees and constituents become involved in collaborative endeavors, it is understandable and desirable that they exercise greater leadership, decision-making, and organizational influence. However, as Crow and Matthews suggest, school administrators may feel reluctant to relinquish some of their influence, authority, or control—especially if they must be accountable for the independent decisions and actions of others. That is, if teachers and others are going to expand their influence and leadership through collaborative work, they must also assume responsibility and accountability for their decisions and actions. Collaborative work groups must be willing to answer to parents, school board members, and others for their collective decisions and actions rather than expecting school administrators to take a protective role, supporting their actions under all circumstances.

This makes an uncomfortable transition for both collaborative work groups and administrators. Administrators have long been expected to "support" teachers when they face criticism from or conflict with parents, students, board members, or other community groups. For the most part, this support has meant running interference for or protecting a single teacher from criticism or complaint about his/her individual actions in the classroom. However, as collaborative work groups expand their leadership roles, spheres of influence, and range of responsibilities, school administrators may be expected to support decisions of which they have only minimal knowledge or over which they have little control. Also, teachers may be uncomfortable stepping up to the plate of public scrutiny. However, the dynamics of shared leadership—especially between school administrators and collaborative school groups—cannot be successful if those who make decisions are unwilling to take responsibility or be accountable for those decisions. Increased collaborative leadership and influence *require* increased responsibility and accountability.

Balance of Influence versus Overcontrol
or Underinvolvement of Members

A certain degree of conflict is inherent to collaborative work. Several authors have discussed the dynamics of conflict in earlier chapters (e.g., Barott and Raybould, chap. 3, Galvin, chap. 4, Hart, chap. 6, Crow, chap. 8). Conflict can occur over a host of issues, including differences in educational philosophies, values, goals, instructional techniques, work priorities, role expectations, and so on. However, one area that seems to have particularly strong potential for conflict is the imbalance of inputs and influence by collaborative group members. When there is a reasonable balance of inputs among the participating parties, there is much greater potential for effective problem solving, decision making, work effort, and work results; this enhanced group effectiveness tends to correspond with group harmony. However, collaborative groups may include parties who tend to exercise too much control over the group's actions or, conversely, offer little input or support for group activities.

"Controlling members" as well as "shirking members" create critical problems for collaborative groups and their work.

There may be many reasons that members engage in either controlling behavior or shirking behavior. A lack of trust may explain some members' behavior (see Galvin, chap. 4, Evans-Stout, chap. 7). When group members do not trust the intentions, competence, or motivations of other members, they may tend to try to control the direction and decisions of the group, or they may withdraw from the group to the degree possible. Controlling or shirking behavior may also reflect members' general lack of commitment to change toward a more collaborative school. Whether members behave in an aggressive or passive-aggressive fashion, their intentions may be to resist *change* and to *persist* with the current school organization and processes. Either type behavior (controlling or shirking) can threaten the survival and effectiveness of the group, upsetting the balance of inputs among members and potentially alienating other group members.

An imbalance in member involvement and participation in group activities is a touchy interpersonal process to address and remedy. However, failure to openly and directly deal with the problem will only allow the group dynamics to spin more out of balance. (The image that comes to my mind is a washing machine on the spin cycle with an imbalanced load of heavy wet towels inside.) Although there is risk involved for a group to openly address any type of interpersonal problem, feelings of trust and commitment are more likely to increase with candid and open exchanges than with continued unspoken assumptions and attributions operating. Often a neutral outside party can be helpful in facilitating these types of direct and honest communication.

CLOSING COMMENTS

At this point, I hope that readers can appreciate the complexity that accompanies school collaboration efforts. The purpose of this book was to articulate some of the issues that must be considered when embarking on collaborative work. Collaborative school architects much consider many factors, starting with the *organizational structure* of schools. How do existing structures enhance or inhibit the likelihood of effective collaboration? For example, do school rewards, incentives, communication networks, and coordination tools facilitate or undermine potential collaborative efforts? How can these and other school structures be modified to be more consistent with the goals of collaboration?

Next, how should the *change process* be approached? Is first order change or second order change more appropriate? What "persistence" dynamics can be expected, worked with, and worked through as a natural part of the change process? What are the anticipated *costs and benefits* of collaboration? How can organizational structures and group processes be designed to minimize costs in relation to collaboration's benefits or resource gains? To what degree can collaboration among teachers and other school professionals enhance student learning and favorable school experiences? If so, how can *teachers' work be redesigned* to encourage work group effectiveness? What work group structures, processes, and contextual factors can be developed to increase work group effectiveness to best serve the needs of students? Similarly, how can other education or social service agency professionals' work be aligned more closely with teachers' work for the purpose of better serving students? How can these professionals learn to overcome their separate *role socialization* to work effectively together? What are the anticipated effects of school collaboration on *teaching and learning* and *school leadership*? What kinds of *professional preparation and development* are needed to help educators learn to work collaboratively?

The difficulty with implementing any collaborative effort is that all of these factors must be considered in combination—as interacting factors. These multiple considerations or perspectives do not operate in isolation of one another; a holistic approach is required. Therein lies the complexity of school collaboration. The salience of one factor relative to another may vary depending on the particular school, collaborative effort, point in time, or key players involved. Thus, few of us would be willing to offer strict formulas for effective collaboration.

However, we do offer two strong and resounding recommendations to those embarking on collaborative school efforts. First, the primary reason that schools should engage in collaborative work is to enhance the benefits and services to students. All other purposes of collaboration are subordinate to that of effectively meeting students' needs. Second, collaborative work structures and processes should be developed around the teaching-learning process. Improved teaching and learning should be the highest priority and focus of collaborative schools.

REFERENCES

Ogawa, R. T. (1996). Bridging and buffering relations between parents and schools. *UCEA Review*, 37 (2), pp. 2–3, 12–13. University Park, PA.

Smylie, M.A., Lazarus, V., & Brownlee-Conyers, J. (1996). Instructional outcomes of school- based participative decisionmaking. *Educational Evaluation and Policy Analysis*, 18, 181–198.

ABOUT THE AUTHORS

Bob L. Johnson, Jr. is Assistant Professor of Educational Administration at the University of Utah, where he teaches graduate courses in organizational theory and politics of education. Johnson's scholarship chronicles a decade or more of educational reform in the state of Utah and analyzes organizational structures and learning outcomes of reform initiatives. Most recently, the author's research has focused on the relationship between decentralized governance structures in school organizations and various measures of school effectiveness.

James E. Barott was Assistant Professor of Educational Administration at the University of Utah, where he taught graduate courses in organizational change and development, qualitative research methods, and organizational theory. His research addresses organizational change and development and the micropolitics of educational organizations. He is currently Associate Professor at the University of Texas-Pan American.

Rebecca Raybould is a Ph.D. student and Research Assistant in Educational Administration at the University of Utah. She holds an M.Ed. degree in Educational Studies with an emphasis in teaching and learning strategies. She draws upon her teaching and organizational change experiences from her work in the corporate business world as a systems analyst and a manager.

Patrick F. Galvin is Associate Professor of Educational Administration at the University of Utah, where he teaches courses in education finance, economics of education, and analytic methods for decision making. He has a well-developed line of research in organizational economics and inter-agency collaboration. Currently he works on the board of several collaborative organizations within the state of Utah. Galvin is co-director, with David Sperry, of the University of Utah's Educational Policy Center.

Diana G. Pounder is Professor and Associate Chair of Educational Administration at the University of Utah, where she teaches graduate courses in school personnel administration and quantitative research methods. Her scholarship in personnel administration includes focus on equity issues in employee selection and compensation. Her most recent research emphasis is on organizational leadership and teacher teams. She also draws upon her experience as a middle school principal who transformed a school from a traditional teacher work design model to a teacher team/work group model.

Ann Weaver Hart is Dean of the Graduate School and Professor of Educational Administration at the University of Utah. For this chapter, she draws on her research on work design in schools; collaborative teaching and problem-solving courses involving educators working as psychologists, counselors, classroom teachers, special educators, and administrators; and work as a school principal. She also has written collaboratively with scholars from other disciplines about inter-role collaboration and their joint graduate teaching experiences.

Karen Evans-Stout was Assistant Professor in the Department of Educational Administration at the University of Utah, where she taught graduate courses in educational evaluation and instructional leadership. She has published and presented research on outcome-based education and the importance of the knowledge base for learning. She is currently Program Coordinator for the teacher leadership program at the University of Minnesota.

Gary M. Crow is Associate Professor of Educational Administration at the University of Utah, where he teaches graduate courses in educational leadership and staff development. Crow has conducted research in several urban areas focusing on school principals and the socialization of principals at both entry and mid-career stages. He has written numerous articles on leadership, the principal, and restructured schools including a monograph on systemic leadership. His scholarship also draws on his prior principalship experience.

Joseph Matthews is Clinical Professor of Educational Administration at the University of Utah, where he teaches a school principalship seminar, supervises administrative interns, and has developed and implemented a training program for mentor principals. He has been involved in the development of programs teaching collaboration for university pre-service preparation and for school district in-service professional development. The course described as an illustration in his chapter is team taught by the author with other college of education professors at the University of Utah. He further draws on his prior experience as a high school principal.

INDEX